# Papering
# & Painting

## Julian Cassell
## Peter Parham

MARSHALL PUBLISHING · LONDON

**A Marshall Edition**
Conceived, edited and designed by
Marshall Editions
The Orangery
161 New Bond Street
London W1Y 9PA

First published in the UK in 2000 by Marshall
Publishing Ltd

ISBN: 1-84028-228-2

Originated in Singapore by Chroma Graphics
Printed and bound in China by Excel Printing

**Project Editor** Felicity Jackson

**Designed by** Martin Lovelock
                & John Round

**Photographer** Tim Ridley

**Illustrations** Chris Forsey

**Project Manager** Nicholas Barnard

**Managing Art Editor** Patrick Carpenter

**Editorial Director** Ellen Dupont

**Art Director** Dave Goodman

**Editorial Coordinator** Ros Highstead

**Production** Anna Pauletti

**Indexer** Hilary Bird

Front cover photography: **John Freeman** (top and
centre) **Elizabeth Whiting & Associates** (bottom
left and bottom right) **Tim Ridley** (bottom centre)
Back cover photography: **Tim Ridley**

## Note

Every effort has been taken to ensure that all
information in this book is correct and compatible with
national standards generally accepted at the time of
publication. This book is not intended to replace the
manufacturer's instructions in the use of their tools or
materials – always follow their safety guidelines. The
author and publisher disclaim any liability, loss, injury or
damage incurred as a consequence, directly or indirectly,
of the use and application of the contents of this book.

*The authors would like
to thank the following
companies for their
assistance in producing
this book:*

Dulux Decorator Centres
Altrincham
Cheshire
WA14 5PG
Tel. 0161 9683000

Dave Marsh Hardware
Fore Street
Castle Cary
Somerset
BA7 7BG
Tel. 01963 350316

The English Stamp
Company
Worth Matravers
Dorset
BH19 3JP
Tel. 01929 439117

The Stencil Store
89 Lower Sloane Street
London
SW1 W8DA
Tel. 0171 823 6700

Polyvine Ltd
Vine House
Rockhampton
Berkeley
Gloucestershire
GL13 9DT
Tel. 01454 261276

Sharpe & Fisher (BS) Ltd
Mill Street
Wincanton
Somerset
BA9 9AP
Tel. 01963 33881

Hewden Plant Hire
Station Road
Bruton
Somerset
BA10 0EH
Tel. 01749 812267

MGR Exports
Station Road
Bruton
Somerset
BA10 0EH
Tel. 01749 812460

Akzo Nobel Decorative
Coatings Ltd
PO Box 37
Crown House
Hollins Road
Darwen
Lancashire
BB3 0BG
Tel. 01254 704951

Bruton Cast Ltd
Unit 1 Riverside
Station Road Industrial
Estate
Bruton
Somerset
BA10 0EH
Tel. 01749 813266

*Further thanks goes to
the following individuals
who supplied props and
general assistance:*

Adele Parham, Emma
Isaacs, John and Margaret
Dearden, Jakki Dearden,
Rob Mahoney, and Julia
Barnard.

All styling for set
photography by Julian
Cassell, Peter Parham, Tim
Ridley and Katrina Moore.

# CONTENTS

# INTRODUCTION

P aper and paint are the primary tools for decorating your home, and creating colour schemes using these essential materials can be very rewarding – both conceiving the actual design ideas and the practical application of these ideas to rooms and surfaces within your home. Decorating is an ideal vehicle for self indulgence since it allows you to express your personal tastes and preferences in a way that is beneficial to your lifestyle by making pleasant surroundings to live in, and beneficial in a practical way by improving the look of your home and adding to its financial value. Experienced decorators and novices alike will benefit from the techniques and advice in the following chapters because there is always room for improvement, whatever the level of your ability. Trying different techniques and finishes, or experimenting with alternative products is all part of the process. Painting and papering provide the finishing touches to your home, so enjoy the process and it will continue to give pleasure for many years.

## CHOOSING COLOUR AND PATTERN

Style is very much a personal issue and the way you choose colours and patterns for your home is based on where you look for inspiration. Most of us have favourite colours and types of design, but moulding these into a finished product suitable for your particular room or rooms can be a daunting process. The best thing is to seek your inspiration from all areas of life; for example, using lifestyle magazines for ideas and fashion hints can be very helpful. Develop these external influences still further by taking note of the kind of things that attract you to certain rooms in other people's houses. Look at the variety of shapes and sizes that you come across in your everyday life, and consider how you could apply them to colour schemes and designs within your home. Devising a scheme can be as simple or as complicated a process as you wish to make it. By taking into account all the different influences open to you, choosing colour and pattern provides an open avenue to fulfilling your desire to create a well decorated and attractive home.

## THE PLANNING PROCESS

The most important part of any papering or painting job is the initial planning stage. The time spent choosing a scheme and preparing the surfaces will always pay dividends by helping to ensure a well-finished product. Chapter 1 provides all the information needed to deal with this stage of the decorating process, demonstrating the most efficient preparatory techniques to use on different surfaces.

## ESSENTIAL PAINTING

Applying paint to walls and woodwork in the correct manner is a vital part of the decorating process. Different painting tools require different techniques, so choosing the tools that suit you, and are appropriate for the job on hand, is a matter of personal preference. Chapter 2 provides detailed instruction on using painting tools in the best way possible to ensure that your painted finish will live up to expectations.

## CREATING EFFECTS

Paint effects are definitely the fun side of painting, as well as being the area that can produce the most dramatic finishes. The whole process of producing these stunning effects is a learning curve, with some of the techniques being more difficult than others. Chapter 3 guides you through the various paint effects, plus some modern variations on the more traditional decorating themes, all of which combine to create an exciting, idea-provoking section of this book.

## PAPERING PRINCIPLES

Chapter 4 explains the principles and basic methods involved in general paper-hanging technique. The success of any papered finish is built on these firm foundations, and progress is dependent on a good grasp of these simple but effective methods. As well as providing instruction on paper hanging, this section also shows you how to solve all the common wallpapering problems experienced by most home decorators.

## AWKWARD AREAS

Most rooms are not completely square, and nearly all have some obstacles that need to be overcome when papering the wall surface. Chapter 5 deals with all these areas and provides clear instruction on the best methods to use, from how to deal with arches to building steady and secure platforms for decorating in stairwells. A good understanding of these methods will stand any decorator in good stead for dealing with any problems and obstacles encountered on a wall surface.

## PAINT AND PAPER COMBINATIONS

Most decorative schemes can be enlivened by combining wallpaper and paint to create highly innovative finishes. Chapter 6 discusses the ways of using paper and paint in a scheme, as well as explaining how to apply paintable papers, which give a further option to the home decorator. Combining all these mediums can be a very rewarding process, leading to all sorts of highly original decorative finishes and designs.

## MODERN INNOVATION

As well as perfecting both the simple and more advanced techniques involved in papering and painting your home, it is a good idea to investigate the innovations and developments in the area of home decoration. Manufacturers are constantly trying to produce new and better materials, which are often claimed to be revolutionary and essential for all enthusiasts. Usually the claims are exaggerated, but sometimes new products do make life much easier and they are well worth trying. For example, the introduction of rollers for painting was truly a ground-breaking day! Also, water-based paints are becoming by far the most popular paints to use because of their improved formula and ease of use. So, be aware of change and try to use it to your advantage – finding a new tool for a job, or even refining old techniques and improving them, can be a very enjoyable part of the paint and papering process.

# PREPARATION AND PLANNING

*Good preparation before you start any decorating task will make the entire process easier and help you achieve the best possible finish. As well as the physical preparation required to make surfaces ready for decoration, it is also essential to plan your decoration. Choosing colour schemes and deciding on finishes is the vital first step of any decorating job; take time to think over all the options before making any final decisions. This chapter covers all these aspects and provides a firm base or starting point on which to build your painting and papering technique – it discusses the many different surfaces in the home and the best way to prepare them for decoration.*

# TOOLS AND EQUIPMENT

W hatever the decorating task, the correct tools for the job will help you achieve the best possible finish, so don't compromise on the equipment requirements. Using tools specifically designed for a particular job also makes that job far easier to carry out. Not all the decorating tools are required for every task – a papering and painting toolkit can be built up gradually over time, according to need.

## PAINTING EQUIPMENT

Radiator roller

Fitch

Roller cage and sleeve

Mini-roller

Extension pole

Paint roller tray

Window scraper

Small paint pad

Paintbrushes

Filling knife

Paint pad

Paint pad and application bracket

Shavehook

Glass shield

Dust mask

Hot-air gun

Paint kettle

Sander

# WALLPAPERING EQUIPMENT

Pasting table

Seam roller

Craft knife

Bucket

Wallpaper scorer    Tape measure    Abrasive paper

Pasting brush

Wallpaper trough

Sealant dispenser

Paper-hanging brush    Caulking blade    Sponge

Spirit level

Paper-hanging scissors

Rubber gloves

Stepladder

Steam stripper    Goggles

# CHOOSING A COLOUR SCHEME

C hoosing the colour scheme for a room can be a difficult process because so many factors have to be taken into consideration. Personal taste should always be the main factor, but you also need to have some awareness of the effects of different colours and patterns and take these into account. Allow plenty of time at this vital planning stage and consider all the available options and alternatives before making a final decision.

## THE COLOUR WHEEL

All colours are created from the three primary colours, red, yellow and blue, with secondary and tertiary colours derived from these. The colour wheel below gives an indication of the way in which different colours relate to each other – opposite colours contrast, while near colours complement each other.

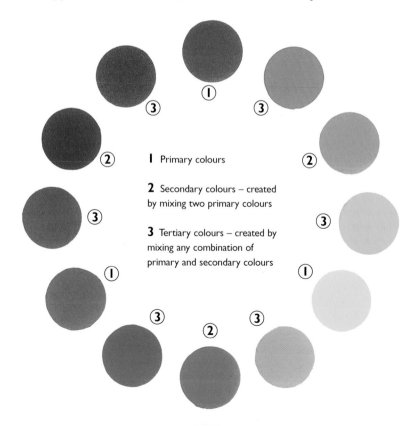

1 Primary colours

2 Secondary colours – created by mixing two primary colours

3 Tertiary colours – created by mixing any combination of primary and secondary colours

**LIGHT AND COLOUR**
Whenever possible, colour choices should be checked in both natural daylight and artificial light because some colours change dramatically in different lights.

## THE EFFECTS OF COLOUR

- There is no need to become to involved in complicated colour chemistry when creating a scheme, simply use the colour wheel as a guide.
- Complementary colours: the colours that complement each other sit opposite each other on the colour wheel. Combined in a colour scheme, they produce a very balanced effect.
- Adjacent colours: using colours that appear next to each other on the colour wheel creates a very harmonious scheme with no strong clashes of colour.

**BALANCED SCHEME**
A balanced scheme is one in which no one colour dominates the others. In this room, the bright colours complement each other.

## PLANNING A SCHEME

- The actual planning of a scheme is affected by a number of factors, such as whether you are using paint or wallpaper. Wallpaper generally means that pattern will play a major role in the scheme, whereas paint on its own places more emphasis on large areas of a single colour.
- Focusing the scheme: choosing one colour and building the rest of the decorating around it is a common method of producing a scheme.
- Practicality: busy areas of the home receive the most wear and tear –

make sure the scheme you choose will stand up to the treatment it is likely to receive. Expensive delicate wallpapers, for example, are not ideal for bathrooms or kitchens.
- Furniture and surroundings: a colour scheme does not just involve walls, ceilings and woodwork – flooring, furniture and other accessories will all have to fit into the final plan. Consider the colour and design of all these items and check whether they will complement the ideas and colour changes you have in mind.

# PROPERTIES OF PAINT AND PAPER

O nce colours and designs have been chosen, it is essential to have some understanding of the actual make-up of decorating materials in order to judge whether a particular surface is suitable for the finish you want to achieve. Some wallpapers, for example, require specific treatment; whereas with paint, it is important to apply the correct type for the surface in question.

Types of paint: the majority of paints can be divided into two main types – the more traditional oil-based/solvent-based paints and the water-based/acrylic paints. Oil-based paints are much less user-friendly because of their longer drying times and unpleasant smell. They are also more harmful to the environment. For these reasons, water-based paints have become very popular and they now dominate the market place. Oil-based paints used to be considered the most hard-wearing, but in recent years water-based paints have improved so much that they now match their oil-based counterparts. However, in certain cases, it is better to use oil-based paints, and these situations are discussed in the following chapters.

## PAINT AND ITS USES

- Primer: this is used to seal surfaces before applying further coats of paint. All bare wood, metal and other untreated surfaces require priming, otherwise subsequent coats will not adhere properly.
- Undercoat: this is any coat of paint that comes between the primer and top coat on a new surface. It is also used on old painted surfaces before a top coat is applied.
- Eggshell: finishing paint that provides a dull, almost matt finish. Ideal on wood and can be used on walls for a hard-wearing finish. Eggshell hybrids bridge the gap between a totally matt finish and a high gloss one.

- Gloss: the hardest-wearing top coat paint, providing a shiny finish. Ideal for wood, but not walls.
- Emulsion: many different varieties are available. Some include vinyl, which produces a slightly shiny wipeable finish. Various proprietary emulsions have specific properties, ranging from completely flat finishes to more textured ones. Easy to use and ideal for all large surface areas.
- Natural finishes: these translucent paints are used to highlight the natural grain of wood. Stains and varnishes are the best-known ones, although there are now many other different varieties of finish available.

## WALLPAPER AND ITS USES

- Plain lining paper: off-white in colour, lining paper is used as the base for all wallpaper finishes. It should be applied to walls and then allowed to dry thoroughly before wallpaper is applied over the top. Lining paper can also be painted – it is often used as an alternative to plastering wall surfaces that are uneven because it smooths over these areas and creates a sound surface for painting.
- Paintable papers: as well as lining papers, there are other types of textured wallpaper specifically designed to be painted. Woodchip paper is the most common example.
- Vinyl: this is a very popular wallpaper which is ideal in all areas of the home, providing an easily wipeable surface. The hard-wearing properties vary according to the grade of vinyl.
- Standard patterned wallpaper: again, very popular and manufactured in many different varieties. Because it is not as hard-wearing as vinyl, it is best used in areas like the living room, rather than the kitchen.
- Hand-made and hand-painted paper: this is only produced in quantity by specialist suppliers. Often extremely expensive, but it can produce a breathtaking finish.
- Proprietary variations: there are various other papers that may require the use of a specific paste. Always follow the manufacturer's guidelines in such cases, especially if using natural papers such as silk or hessian.

Types of wallpaper: the vast majority of wallpaper falls into two categories: vinyl and standard patterned paper. Vinyl is more hard-wearing because of its protective coating. Most wallpaper is hung on the wall using the same technique, though there are small refinements with some papers. The important difference between wallpapers is the method by which they are pasted (see Chapter 4). The main thing at this stage is choosing the correct paper for the purpose (see above), and understanding the effect that a finish may have on a room.

### CAUTION

Decorating materials sometimes contain hazardous chemicals that can be damaging to health. Always obey the basic rules of decorating by ensuring good ventilation in the work area, and follow the manufacturer's safety guidelines for whichever product you are using.

# PREPARING THE ROOM

The first stage of the practical side of room decoration is preparing the room itself. Having plenty of space to work in and ensuring that there are no obstacles in the way, is essential when carrying out any papering or painting task. As well as making it easier to carry out the work, a well-prepared room speeds up the job and ensures that it is completed with the least inconvenience in the quickest time possible.

## CLEARING THE ROOM

Ideally, everything should be removed from the room you are planning to decorate. If this is not possible, there are a number of compromises you can make.

- Carpets: if the carpet is going to be changed, this is the time to remove it. Otherwise, it can be taken up and relaid after decoration, or dust sheets can be put down to protect it during the work. If using dust sheets, run masking tape around the skirting board/carpet junction, to protect the carpet from paint overspray.

- Furniture: remove as much furniture as possible. A few heavy items can be moved into the centre of the room and covered, but always ensure that all wall surfaces are clear of obstructions.

- Ornaments: take as many as possible out of the room and store them elsewhere until the decorating is finished. Some larger items can be put underneath furniture in the centre of the room, but the majority of items should always be removed from the working area.

Covering furniture: use transparent polythene dust sheets for the furniture. These protect totally from paint overspray, but allow you to see what is under the dust sheet, which is important if any of the items are breakable.

Covering floors: always use good quality fabric dust sheets on the floor – cheaper ones let paint through – and make sure they are laid right up to the wall.

# IDENTIFYING PROBLEMS

All surfaces require preparation before decoration; once the room is clear, it is much easier to identify the areas that require the most preparation.

Ceiling cracks that follow a relatively straight path are often caused by movement of the building boards used in the ceiling construction. Where this occurs, line your ceilings as the cracks will return quickly if you only use filler.

In new buildings, cracks along ceiling/wall junctions are generally due to settlement. In older buildings, if the cracks widen, you may need professional advice to check for subsidence. Most cracks are due to slight building movement and should be filled with a flexible filler.

Cracks at the corners of windows and doors are often due to slight movement when opening and closing them. Fill with all-purpose filler.

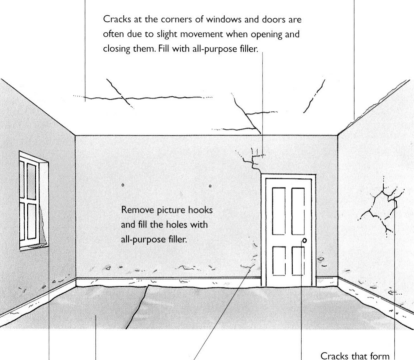

Remove picture hooks and fill the holes with all-purpose filler.

Look out for areas of damp, especially around windows. These may need exterior treatment before decoration begins. Alternatively, the damp could be a result of condensation.

Scrapes and knocks are part of everyday life. Use all-purpose filler to make good.

Be sure to cover the entire floor with dust sheets.

If the door furniture is to be replaced, now is the time to remove it. Fill redundant screw holes in readiness for fitting the new door furniture.

Cracks that form irregular shapes such as this often suggest that the plaster may be blowing away from the wall. Tap it with your hand to see if it sounds hollow. If this is the case, the plaster in that area will need to be removed and patch plaster applied.

# PREPARING WALLS

M aking sure that wall surfaces are smooth before the application of paint or paper plays an important part in achieving a good finish. Lumps and bumps or divots in the surface of the wall will be accentuated by the new decoration and spoil the overall look. The amount of preparation will depend on the wear and tear that the walls have received since the last time they were decorated. In many cases, a light sand, clean down and some filler in one or two places may be all that is required. If damage is more extensive, it may be necessary to replaster some areas. Remember that if your walls have old wallpaper coverings, they must be removed before further preparation can start (see pages 24-25).

## PATCH PLASTERING

Plastering is a highly skilled trade and, as a rule, attempting to plaster entire rooms on your own should be avoided – it makes far more sense to employ professional help. However, small localized areas that require only slightly more than simple, all-purpose filler can be patch plastered – a job well within the capability of the home decorator. Make sure you buy 'one-coat plaster', which is easier to work with than the more traditional two-coat plastering systems. Mixed to the manufacturer's guidelines, it takes on the consistency of a stodgy, but easily workable paste.

1 Dust away any loose debris from the sides of the hole and dampen the area with a PVA solution (one part PVA to five parts water). Use a plastering float to press the plaster firmly into the hole while drawing the float across the face of the entire filled hole.

2 Smooth the surface of the plaster and allow it to dry slightly (for about 30 minutes). Then wet the face of the float with water and smooth the plaster surface again. Continue 'polishing' the surface of the plaster with the float until a smooth and flush finish is produced.

## REPAIRING A PLASTERBOARD WALL

Plasterboard or dry-lined walls require a different technique in order to fill any holes in the surface layer of the plasterboard. Because the wall is hollow, plaster or filler will simply fall inside the wall cavity if it is applied directly to the hole. For large holes, a section of plasterboard may need to be replaced; for smaller holes, the technique demonstrated here is the ideal solution.

1 Use a craft knife to cut away any loose material from around the edge of the hole.

2 Cut a new piece of plasterboard, slightly larger than the hole. Drill a hole in the centre of it and thread a piece of string through it, knotting it on one side. On the opposite side, spread all-purpose adhesive around the edge of the piece of board.

3 Holding the string, 'post' the board through the hole and move it into place on the reverse side of the hole. Tie the string to a small piece of wood to hold the board in place.

4 Leave the adhesive to dry then cut the string and wood away. Fill the gap in the wall with plaster.

**Minor hole filling:** very small divots and holes in any wall can be filled with all-purpose filler applied with a filler knife. Where there are several holes close to each other, a caulking blade can be used to sweep filler over the entire area, filling all the holes with maximum speed and minimum effort.

# PREPARING WOOD

Wood tends to act as the frame to the wall decoration and plays an equal part in the overall look of the room. If a professional finish is to be achieved, wood preparation is as important as wall preparation. Wood surfaces can present more problems than walls, as moulded corners and edges can make filling and preparation a slightly more intricate task than the broader open surfaces of the walls.

## BEFORE FILLING

Before filling the dents and holes in wooden surfaces, you need to deal with any protruding areas. This takes a little time, but it helps to ensure a smooth finished product.

1 Knock in any nails that are sticking out of the wood surface, using a hammer and punch.

2 Bumps on old painted surfaces can be removed by running a scraper along the face of the wood.

## FILLING FLAT SURFACES

All-purpose filler can be used to fill flatter wooden surfaces. Make sure that it is mixed into a smooth, creamy consistency, with no lumps or dry areas.

1 Filler shrinks as it dries, so fill holes so that the filler sits slightly 'proud' of the hole's edges.

2 Once it is dry, the filler can be sanded by hand, or with an electric sander, as shown here.

# FILLING JOINTS AND CRACKS

Cracks are commonly found at the junction between wood and walls, as well as in the jointing system of wooden items – such as the edges of panels in doors, or the point at which the architrave joins onto the main part of the door frame. In all these cases, you need to use a flexible filler that can cope with the slight movement which most of these areas experience. Flexible filler, or caulk, is dispensed from a tube using a sealant gun.

1 Cut the tube nozzle to a size that will allow a thin bead of filler. Pull the sealant gun trigger to allow a thin bead of filler to run along the joint, keeping even pressure on the trigger while guiding the nozzle.

2 While the filler is still wet, smooth along the bead surface with a wet finger, to give an even and neat finish, ready for painting.

# UNPAINTED WOOD

After filling as necessary, you must seal any wood that has not been painted before. This is a two-part process involving the use of knotting solution and primer.

2 Once the knotting solution has dried, seal the entire wood surface with primer, making sure it is totally covered and that the primer is well brushed into the wood.

1 Brush knotting solution into all knots in the bare wood. This seals in any resin and prevents it from bleeding through the subsequent coats of paint, which would spoil the surface.

## NATURAL WOOD ALTERNATIVES

For natural wood finishes, the wood must be sanded smooth as normal, but use stainable fillers to deal with holes – knotting solution and primer are not usually used on natural wood finishes. Alternative methods are shown on pages 38-39.

# PREPARING OTHER SURFACES

As well as walls and wood, there are other surfaces that require preparation before they can be decorated. The most common of these are metal surfaces and man-made surfaces such as plastic and melamine. With the correct preparation, nearly all of these can be painted to fit in with your chosen colour scheme.

## METAL SURFACES

The preparation of a metal surface depends very much on the type of metal and whether it has been painted before. There are various all-purpose primers that can be used as a base on most metals, although in many cases it is better to use a primer designed for the specific metal.

## PAINTING RADIATORS

Radiators are one of the more common metal surfaces in the home, and they can be painted to either complement or contrast with the rest of the decoration in the room. Because most modern radiators are supplied ready coated, changing their colour is a simple process.

### PRIMING METALS

- Copper: there is no need to prime copper – undercoats and top coats can be applied directly to cleaned and sanded surfaces.
- Iron and steel: because these metals are ferrous, they are prone to corroding or rusting. On older surfaces, any old flaky material must be removed. Use a proprietary metal primer before applying further coats of paint.
- Aluminium: generally, proprietary aluminium primers can be used to secure a base coat which may then be painted with top coats.

1 Use a fine-grade abrasive paper to lightly sand the surface of the whole radiator.

2 Make sure that the radiator is turned off and cool before you paint it. Apply undercoat and leave it to dry, then paint with a top coat.

## MELAMINE

Kitchen unit surfaces are often made of melamine, which is not designed to be painted. However, with recent product developments, you can now paint it, as long as the correct surface preparation is carried out.

1 Clean the melamine surface with a mild detergent solution, rinse with clean water and then allow it to dry completely.

2 Sand the entire melamine surface with a fine-grade abrasive paper.

3 Apply a proprietary surface preparation solution to the melamine, wiping it onto all areas with a clean cotton cloth.

4 Wipe off the excess solution with another cloth and allow to dry. The melamine surface is now ready to accept an undercoat, followed by top coats of paint.

### OTHER UNUSUAL SURFACES

Various other surfaces around the home can also be painted, though you should always check the manufacturer's guidelines to see if a particular paint is suitable for a specific surface.

• Tiles: clean and sand tiles then apply a proprietary tile primer before painting them.
• Textured ceiling coatings: with a previously painted surface, apply emulsion paint in the usual way. For a new textured coating, seal the surface with diluted emulsion paint and leave to dry before applying further coats of paint.
• Glass: clean thoroughly and then use proprietary glass paints to create a decorative effect.
• Plastic: clean thoroughly then apply top coats directly to the surface.

# STRIPPING PAPER

I t is always best to remove old layers of paper before carrying out any redecoration. However secure the old paper may appear on the wall, once it is painted or wallpapered over any defects will begin to show and these will ruin the look of the newly decorated room.

### REMOVING THE WORST

Begin by simply removing those layers of paper that come away from the wall surface with relative ease – starting with any loose seams.

1 The top layer of paper can often be pulled away from its backing, especially when it is vinyl paper.

2 Use the scraper to get behind the paper and remove areas that are no longer stuck to the wall surface.

### SIMPLE STRIPPING

If paper is still stuck to the wall after the top layer has been removed, use warm water to strip it off. Do not use this method if vinyl paper is still on the wall, as the water will simply run off the surface.

1 Apply plenty of warm water to the paper. Allow the water to soak in and make the paper bubble.

2 Scrape away the damp, loosened paper, trying not to dig the edges of the scraper into the wall surface.

## USING A STEAM STRIPPER

For stubborn areas of paper, a steam stripper is the best removal tool. The design of steam strippers varies, but in general they have a large water-heating reservoir that boils the water and pushes steam down a connecting pipe into a large plate held against the wallpaper surface.

1 Make sure that the steam stripper is turned off, then fill the reservoir with hot water up to the indicated level. Using hot water speeds up the time it takes for the water to boil. Fit the connecting pipe and turn on the machine.

2 To speed up the process, score the surface of the wallpaper. Use a scorer to make small holes in the top layer of the wallpaper surface so that steam can penetrate behind the paper and speed up its removal.

3 Once the steamer has boiled, hold the steaming plate flat on the wall surface, keeping it in position for several seconds.

4 Move the plate along and remove the previously steamed piece of paper with a scraper. The time this takes depends on the type of paper and the number of layers.

### CAUTION

Always wear protective equipment when using a steam stripper. Both gloves and goggles should be worn to give protection from the steam.

# STRIPPING WOOD

U nlike stripping wallpaper, which is usually a necessity before redecoration, stripping wood is not always essential. However, if you are going to apply a natural wood finish to a previously painted, varnished or stained surface, you need to strip the wood.

### HOT-AIR GUNS

Hot-air guns remove paint by heating up the old paint on the surface. This makes it bubble and loosen its grip so it is easy to scrape away.

Using a hot-air gun: hold the nozzle of the gun close to, but not touching, the painted surface. As soon as the paint begins to lift, scrape it away and move the nozzle to a new area, so that you do not scorch the wood.

| CAUTION |
| --- |
| Wear protective gloves and always read the manufacturer's guidelines before using a hot-air gun. |

### CHEMICAL STRIPPERS

Chemical strippers can be used on paint or natural wood finishes with equal effect. Using this kind of stripper can be a messy business, but it is a very effective way of removing old coatings.

1 Wearing protective gloves, apply chemical stripper liberally to the wood using an old paintbrush.

2 Allow the chemical stripper to react with the old coatings then gently scrape away the residue.

## PASTE STRIPPERS

Paste strippers are a form of chemical stripper that are particularly suitable for intricate areas that require total coating removal. They take longer to react with the old coatings, but are capable of removing a number of layers in one go. They are messy, so make sure that all areas are covered with dust sheets.

1 Apply the stripper to the surface using a scraper or filling knife. Cover the area to be stripped with an even layer of the paste and leave it on for up to 24 hours to allow it to react with the surface.

2 Use a scraper to peel away the paste and reveal the bare wooden surface below. The stripper works by both dissolving the paint or other coating and lifting the layers away.

## CLEANING DOWN

After any stripping process, wood will require a thorough clean before it can be redecorated. As well as washing with water, it may be necessary to use other solvents, depending on the type of stripper you are using. White vinegar is often used to neutralise the stripper residue, but always check the stripper manufacturer's guidelines on specific recommendations.

1 Wearing protective gloves, wash the entire surface to remove the remnants of previous coatings and any stripper residue.

2 Any ingrained areas of paint can be removed by rubbing a small ball of fine-grade steel wool across the affected area.

# SEALING SURFACES

O nce surfaces have been stripped and cleaned, you may need to seal them before they will accept paint or paper. In addition to the wood, metal and miscellaneous surfaces discussed in this chapter, walls, ceilings and the larger areas of the room as a whole need sealing to stabilize them before they are decorated.

## SEALING CHECKLIST

- Previously wallpapered walls: once the paper has been stripped, the walls should be filled and prepared as normal. The surface should then be sealed with a PVA solution (one part PVA to five parts water). If wallpaper is going to be used, the walls must be lined first. Walls that are going to be painted, may require lining first if they are very rough.
- Previously painted walls: after filling and preparing, walls can be painted immediately. If they are to be wallpapered, apply a PVA solution (one part PVA to five parts water) to the surface before lining..
- Previously lined walls: ones that have been painted can be painted again after general preparation. Wallpaper can be applied directly to a wall as long as the lining paper is stuck down. However, it is better to seal the walls with PVA solution (one part PVA to five parts water) first.
- New plastered walls: they should be sealed with a dilute emulsion (10 parts paint to one part water) before further coats are applied. For wallpaper, walls should be prepared and sealed with PVA solution (one part PVA to five parts water), or dilute wallpaper paste (mixed as per manufacturer's guidelines for size) before lining.
- New dry-lined walls: these should be treated like new plastered walls.

## DEALING WITH STUBBORN STAINS

Standard primers and sealants cannot deal with all the stains that appear on walls and woodwork in the home. Sometimes a more robust form of sealant is required to deal with any areas that continue to bleed a stain through the decorated surface.

Using a stain blocker: apply two or three light coats of aerosol stain blocker to stubborn areas of staining that refuse to disappear, even after normal sealing or priming. Decorate the surface as usual.

# PAINTING TECHNIQUES

*When it comes to actually applying paint to the walls, painting technique is often considered with a certain amount of indifference, an attitude that can lead to mistakes which are not easy to rectify. Having prepared surfaces thoroughly, the actual painting part of decorating can be very enjoyable as long as you take the time to ensure that paint is applied correctly. Modern tools make painting a relatively straightforward job, but there are lots of ways of applying paint and it is important to choose an appropriate method for the surface in question and the finish you are trying to achieve.*

# WHAT TOOLS TO USE WHERE

**2**

Different painting tools are designed for particular surfaces, although some tools can be used for more than one type of surface. Most home decorators develop preferences for certain tools and tend to use their favourites as much as possible. However, there are some points that are worth considering when choosing the tools for the job, as they can affect the speed and efficiency of the work.

## CHOOSING TOOLS

The table below sets out the advantages and disadvantages of available painting equipment, to help you select the right tools for the particular decorating job that you are planning.

| PAINTING EQUIPMENT | |
|---|---|
| Brushes | These are the most versatile of all decorating tools, manufactured in all shapes and sizes, and designed for every possible need. Pure bristle brushes are still the best quality, although some of the modern synthetic fibre brushes are constantly improving in their performance – especially for use with water-based paints. Brushes can be used successfully in all areas, although for large expanses of ceiling or walls other methods provide much quicker coverage. |
| Rollers | These are ideal for dealing with large open areas, covering surfaces quickly and with great efficiency. They are manufactured in sheepskin (the best quality) and synthetic materials. Sizes range from 45 cm (18 in) down to 2.5 cm (1 in), so it is possible to find the right size roller for any job. |
| Paint pads | These are the direct competition to rollers, as they have very similar properties – it's usually a matter of personal preference. Paint pads create far less mess than rollers and there is some suggestion that they are much more efficient on paint use than rollers. |
| Sprayers | These are very successful at covering large surfaces quickly, but the mess created, and the amount of masking off that is required, often makes them too inconvenient. They are useful for large areas of uninterrupted wallspace, otherwise they are more suited to industrial painting. However, aerosol spray paints are becoming increasingly popular – they are easily directed into inaccessible areas and require no cleaning as they are simply thrown away when empty. |

# AREAS OF USE

The illustration below shows the different areas of a standard room design and indicates which painting tools are most suitable to use.

**2**

Radiators can be painted with a brush or sprayed with an aerosol. Use a radiator roller to paint behind them.

Walls and ceilings are ideal for large rollers or large paint pads. Paint pads tend to cause less mess. However, it will still be necessary to cut in around the edges of walls and ceilings using a 5-7.5 cm (2-3 in) brush or small paint pad.

Doors can be painted with mini-rollers, but the panel edges and architrave need finishing with a 2.5-5 cm (1-2 in) brush.

Skirting board can be painted with a medium-sized paint pad or a 2.5-5 cm (1-2 in) paintbrush.

Wall alcoves and window reveals are normally too small to accommodate a roller and need to be painted with a 7.5 cm (3 in) paintbrush or a medium-sized paint pad.

Window and door furniture that require painting should be removed and sprayed with aerosol paint. If you don't want to spray with an aerosol, use a small paintbrush or fitch.

## KEEPING UP-TO-DATE

It is worth being aware of new paint tools that come on the market as the manufacturers constantly vary shape and design of painting tools in an effort to improve their performance and, ultimately, the finish they produce. Be careful, though, because it is very easy to fall into the trap of buying gimmicky tools, which sometime promise more than they are capable of delivering.

# BRUSHES

T he correct technique for using a brush varies slightly according to the surface being painted and the type of paint that you are using. Make sure that the brush is in good condition with no loose bristles that could moult and end up on the painted surface.

## WALL TECHNIQUE

To save time, use a relatively large brush when painting walls. However, bear in mind that if your brush is too large, it will be heavy and make your wrist tired, and this may affect your efficiency.

1 Apply the paint in random strokes across the wall, allowing the bristles of the brush to spread the paint as evenly as possible.

2 Once a small area of wall has been painted, without reloading the brush, stroke the bristles lightly across the painted surface to blend in any visible brushmarks in the paint. This process is known as 'laying off'.

3 Use a smaller brush to cut in around the edges of walls, allowing the extreme edge of the brush to 'bead' the paint precisely along the wall/ceiling junction.

### CUTTING IN

Cutting in is a technique for finishing off around edges, such as those between a wall and ceiling, or the wall and a door frame.

# WOOD TECHNIQUE

The same aim of producing a smooth finish applies to painting wood, but the technique varies slightly from that used for walls. If you are using an oil-based paint, make sure that you apply a few more strokes to each paint application so the paint is thoroughly 'brushed out', otherwise it may run or drip.

1 Use a smaller brush for wood application as the work always tends to be more detailed. Working in small areas, apply vertical strips of paint, loading the brush separately for each strip. For the door shown here, three strips cover the width of the panel in the door. Without reloading the brush, blend the strips together by stroking horizontally across the painted area.

2 Finally, and without reloading the brush, make light vertical strokes over the painted area to remove any brush marks and provide a uniform appearance.

3 For the edges where wood meets walls, such as the skirting board, use a small brush to cut in along the top of the skirting and create a precise line dividing the two colours.

## CLEANING AND STORING BRUSHES

- Temporary storage: wet brushes can be stored temporarily in clingfilm. Brushes with oil-based paint on them can be stored in white spirit.
- Cleaning: water-based paint should be washed out of brushes with mild detergent then the brushes should be rinsed thoroughly under cold water before being allowed to dry. Wash oil-based paint out of brushes with white spirit, allow them to dry then wash with a mild detergent, rinse with water and dry.
- Storage: loosely bind the bristles of the brush with brown paper, secured in place with an elastic band.

# ROLLERS

R ollers vary in texture and size, but all are extremely efficient at covering flat areas easily and evenly. They are most commonly used on walls and ceilings, although smaller ones and roller sleeves with a very smooth pile can be used on some wooden surfaces.

## WALL TECHNIQUE

Large rollers can cover wall surfaces very quickly. Choose a roller sleeve according to the amount of texture you want on the wall – a roller with a thick pile is particularly good if the surface is undulating or uneven. Always load paint evenly onto the roller, being careful not to overload it.

1 Load paint onto the roller then allow the roller to glide over the wall surface in a zig-zag pattern.

2 Reload the roller and fill in the gaps. Allow the unloaded roller to glide gently over the painted area to even up the finish.

## EASY ACCESS

Ingenious designs mean that rollers can get into a variety of different areas with relative ease. This easy accessibility makes the roller a very versatile painting tool that is not confined to straightforward wall spaces.

Gaining height: an extension pole attached to the roller makes it possible to paint the higher areas of a wall without the need for a stepladder. It is also useful for ceilings.

Getting behind: a long-handled radiator roller makes it possible to paint behind radiators without taking them off the wall.

## WOOD TECHNIQUE

Very similar painting techniques apply to wood as to walls, and rollers are becoming increasingly popular for use on many wooden surfaces in the home, with doors at the top of the list. The main reason for this popularity is the speed at which a roller can paint a door compared to the more traditional methods of paint application.

2

1 For panel doors, mini-rollers are ideal for painting all the flat areas on the door surface.

2 Use a paintbrush for the more intricate mouldings of the panel edge.

Painting flush doors: a roller is ideal for painting these as there are no intricate areas to interrupt the progress of the roller across the door's surface.

### CLEANING AND STORING ROLLERS

- Water-based paints: rollers are designed to be used with water-based paints and can be cleaned with a mild detergent solution before rinsing thoroughly with clean water. This can be a lengthy process, especially with long-pile roller heads, but it is essential to make sure all traces of paint are removed from the roller so that it can be used in future to apply different colours. Although sheepskin roller heads are more expensive than synthetic equivalents, they tend to wash out more quickly.

- Temporary storage: rollers can be temporarily stored in clingfilm for several days; they should be washed out before the end of the week.

- Oil-based paint: on the rare occasion that oil-based paint might be used with a roller, it is virtually impossible to clean, and would take far too much white spirit. In this case, it is more sensible to use a cheap roller head and throw it away afterwards.

# PAINT PADS

P aint pads are similar to rollers in that they are designed for covering large surface areas quickly, with relatively little effort and maximum efficiency. Paint pads are flat and rectangular with a large number of tightly packed small fibres, which makes them similar to brushes in the way that they convey paint to surfaces. However, paint pads manage to apply the paint very evenly with one sweep of the pad, rather than a number of different strokes. They come in a range of sizes, with large pads designed for painting walls. The precise nature of pad design often means that relatively large pads can also be used for cutting in around edges.

1 Dip the face of the pad in the paint and use the ribbed part of the paint reservoir to distribute the paint across the pad surface.

2 Remove excess paint from the pad by drawing it across the back edge of the paint reservoir.

3 Apply paint to the wall using uniform slightly overlapping strokes across the surface.

4 Cut in around the wall edges by allowing the extreme edge of the paint pad to run precisely along the wall/ceiling junction.

## WOOD TECHNIQUE

There is very little difference between the technique that is used for walls and the one that is used for wood, except that the size of the paint pad needs to be reduced for painting wood. Small paint pads are far more versatile than mini-rollers are for getting into the detailed parts of wooden surfaces, and they are capable of painting all but the most intricate of areas.

1   A small pad is ideal for cutting in along the window rebates next to the glass surface. The frame of the pad can be used to guide the fibres precisely along the wood/glass junction.

2   The same pad can be used to continue around the outer edge of the window frame, and to cut in along the wall edge.

3   Medium-sized pads are ideal for painting a skirting board, but make sure that the profile of the skirting board is not too detailed for the pad surface to mould into.

### CLEANING AND STORING PAINT PADS

Paint-pad fibres are very small, which means that the pad itself retains little paint once unloaded. Because the fibres dry very quickly, they must be cleaned immediately after use.

- For water-based paints: remove the pad from its frame and wash it out with mild detergent, then rinse with clean water.
- For oil-based paints: it is nearly impossible to remove all traces of

paint with white spirit, so the pad is best discarded after use.

- Temporary storage: paint pads can be stored temporarily in clingfilm, but this can damage the fibres unless they are wrapped up very carefully. Because they wash out easily when using water-based paints, it is always better to clean the pads during any gaps in the work or at the end of the job, as required.

# NATURAL WOOD FINISHES

B rushes are the ideal tool for most finishes that are applied to natural wood. Woodstain, especially, requires brushing into the grain, a process that other decorating tools are unable to produce efficiently. Natural wood finishes differ slightly from paint finishes in that there is no need for priming or knotting the wood (see page 21) before applying the desired finish, although it may take a number of coats of the finish to produce the required look.

## WOODSTAIN

Woodstain is used to give wood a different colour from its natural form. Stain is best used on untreated surfaces because it penetrates deep into the wood, adding colour and bringing out the natural grain. Dark wood cannot be made lighter, so the wood to be stained must be a fairly light colour to begin with.

1 When applying stain, always follow the natural grain of the wood. Make sure that it is applied evenly because drips or areas of over-application will show once it is dry.

2 Treat different sections of the wood as separate entities, taking care to cut in precisely along all the divisions – any overlaps of stain will show through the finish.

Filling holes: use stainable fillers when dealing with holes in natural wood. Alternatively, mix a little of the stain you are using with some all-purpose filler to provide a precise match.

# VARNISHING

Varnish is a decorative as well as protective finish, which can be bought in anything from matt to high-gloss varieties. It can be applied directly to bare wood or over some stains to act as a further protective layer. Traditionally, varnish was transparent; nowadays, coloured varieties are readily available.

1 Varnish should be applied with the grain, in the same way as woodstain, and brushed well into the wood's surface.

2 Bare wood should be given at least three coats of varnish. Let each coat of varnish dry and sand it lightly before applying the next coat.

## OTHER TREATMENTS

Although stain and varnish are by far the most popular methods of treating bare wood, there are other alternatives that provide equally impressive finishes.

- Stain/Varnish: this all-purpose finish combines both stain and varnish finishes in one product. Apply in the usual way with a paintbrush.
- Scandinavian oil: this is ideal for hardwoods as it penetrates deep into the wood and nourishes it. Apply with a brush and buff it with clean, cotton rags.
- Wax: the most traditional of all natural wood finishes, apply the wax with a cloth. When it has dried, buff it off to reveal the natural beauty of the wood. The one drawback is that waxed surfaces need to be recoated regularly to maintain their sheen.

Combining stain and varnish: you can extend the life of a stained surface, and increase the depth of the finish, by giving it a coat of varnish once the stain has dried.

# FINISHING TOUCHES

O nce all the major areas in a room have been painted, it is important to pay attention to the more detailed places that may not initially appear to require any decoration, such as window and door. These finishing touches ensure that the decoration is as good as possible.

## PAINTING DETAIL

Painting the smaller features in a room requires some variation from the standard techniques already demonstrated in this chapter. As detailed areas have a smaller surface, the tools used to paint them need to be scaled down.

Using aerosols: ideal for getting into intricate areas, aerosol paints can be used on such items as window furniture. Remove them from the window and spray them on an old board. They may require two or three coats to provide an even finish and, as with all spray painting, it is better to apply several thin coats rather than a few thick ones which will make the paint run.

Painting in situ: some older window or door furniture may be quite difficult to remove from their position. In such cases, it is best to use a fitch to paint them while they are in place.

Touching up scrapes: small knocks or imperfections on a newly painted surface should be touched up using a fitch: painting the area with a larger brush can sometimes show up as a rather shadowy finish. As coats of paint should always be applied to complete surface areas rather than just small details, a detailed dab with a small brush will be less visible.

# CLEANING DETAIL

Ensuring that all surfaces are clean after painting will improve the finished look. As well as general cleaning, you may need to remove small paint spills.

**2**

Carpet spills: some paint will always find its way through dust sheets to the carpet below. Small splashes can be removed by scraping the edge of a craft-knife blade across the surface of the paint once it is dry.

Cleaning handles: unpainted window and door furniture may need to have paint splashes removed from their surface. A good polish with a cotton cloth will remove most paint spots, otherwise use a plastic scouring pad.

Glass overspray: paint splashes on glass are normally unavoidable when painting windows. Use a window scraper to remove them.

Electrical sockets: a window scraper is ideal for removing unwanted paint from the surface of electrical sockets. Take care not to dig into the socket.

## CLEANING CHECKLIST

Once the painting is finished, it is a good idea to have a general clean in order to show off the new look.
- Curtains: this is the ideal time to get curtains dry-cleaned, along with cushion covers and any other soft furnishings in the room.

- Windows: clean all windows and other glass.
- Carpets: hire a carpet cleaner to revive older floor coverings.
- Ornaments and accessories: polish the bits and pieces on all surfaces to add to the new look of the room.

# PROBLEM SOLVING

However proficient your painting technique, it is inevitable that you will experience some problems from time to time. Most can be easily rectified and just require some simple preparation before you paint. Some of the most common problems are outlined below.

**Drips:** these mainly occur with oil-based paints, although poor application of water-based paints can also lead to drips or runs. Use a scraper to remove the run, sand the area and repaint.

**Bubbling:** this is normally caused by impurities on the bare surface before paint was applied. Sand the area back and seal or prime as required, before repainting.

**Bleeding knots:** staining on painted woodwork is often caused by a knot bleeding sap through the painted surface. Scrape the sap away and sand back to the knot in question. Apply knotting solution then prime and repaint, as required.

**Blotchy stain:** overlapping brush strokes in a stained surface can lead to a rather blotchy, unsightly finish. Sand the entire section of wood right back to bare wood before restaining.

**Overlapping:** with natural wood finishes, maintain a wet edge; do not overlap wet brush strokes onto a dry area, or the join will be very noticeable. If this occurs, sand the area and reapply finish.

**Dust and dirt:** a rough surface can be caused by poor preparation (lack of sanding) or a build-up of dirt on the brush bristles that is then transferred to the paint surface. Sand the area and repaint.

# SPECIAL PAINT EFFECTS

*Special paint effects are a way of adding further interest and texture to a wall or wooden surface by applying standard decorating paints or transparent glaze in slightly different ways. All these techniques are aimed at producing a finish that is far removed from a flat opaque painted surface. Paint and glaze applied in the ways outlined in this chapter add a totally new dimension to traditional decorating, giving you highly individual, dramatic finishes. Apart from their obvious impact, producing special effects is an incredibly enjoyable and satisfying process, and, however well schooled you become in a particular technique, every piece of decorative work that you produce will be unique and will add a personal touch to the decoration in your home.*

# WHAT PAINT EFFECTS TO USE WHERE

Like paint in general, paint effects can be applied to most surfaces. However, some effects suit particular areas better than others; the box below will help you plan what you want to do.

**3**

## WHERE TO USE PAINT EFFECTS

| PAINT EFFECT | IDEAL AREA | NOTE |
|---|---|---|
| Sponging | Suited to large surface areas, walls, door panels. | Avoid details such as skirting board or architrave. |
| Ragging | Similar to sponging, it is ideal for large surfaces. | Avoid rooms with too many intricate edges or corners. |
| Rag-rolling | Ideal for walls and panels; difficult around the edges. | If possible, fit skirting after the paint effect has been achieved. |
| Dragging and graining | Well suited to woodwork, intricate or plain. | Can be used on walls but difficult to keep an even finish. |
| Colourwashing | One of the simplest effects to create on walls. | Effect is called timber rubbing when done on wood. |
| Liming | Ideal on light-coloured bare wood surfaces. | Similar to timber rubbing, except a lime wax is used. |
| Marbling | Ideal way of breaking up a wall with 'marble' panels. | Difficult effect to achieve, but produces impressive finish. |
| Ageing effects | Excellent way of giving any surface a well lived-in look. | Includes distressing and crackle varnishing processes. |
| Stippling | Ideal for walls and woodwork. | Provides a wonderful textured looking finish, but takes time. |
| Combing | Good on walls as well as panels on woodwork. | Provides a more coarse look than dragging and graining. |
| Stamping | Good on walls. | Good for repeating a design. |
| Stencilling | Reproduces painted designs on any surface. | Good for creating borders, frames and other designs. |

# SPECIALIST EQUIPMENT

P roducing good paint effects requires a few extra decorating tools. Always buy quality tools as the extra expense will pay dividends in the work produced.

Masking tape    Graining rocker    Graining comb

Artist's brush

Natural sponge

Stamp roller

Stencil brushes

Stamps    Hog softener

Craft knife

3

Stippling brush    Protective gloves    Cotton rag    Stencil

## GLAZES

Some paint effects, such as sponging, can be produced with standard emulsion paint, but, in general, most effects are produced by using transparent glaze. Adding colour to glaze creates the translucent, broken-colour finish that is characteristic of most paint effects. Traditionally, glazes were oil-based, but now the vast majority that are available are water-based/acrylic. Water-based glazes tend to be much easier to work with and far more environmentally friendly. All the glazes used in this chapter are water-based, and demonstrate that they can be used to produce any effect you require. Mixing the glaze varies according to the manufacturer's guidelines: generally, it is a simple case of mixing colourizers with the base glaze until you have the desired colour. It is vital to remember that all glazes – and therefore all paint effects – must be applied over a base coat of some description. Emulsion, undercoat and eggshell can all be used, although vinyl silk emulsion is often the manufacturer's choice. A light colour always works best as the base coat, so that subsequent glaze layers show to best effect.

# SPONGING

S ponging is one of the simplest paint effects to produce, while
achieving one of the most dramatic finishes. A natural sponge
is used to make imprints on the wall surface, creating a finish that
combines colour, texture and depth to great effect.

## SPONGING ON

Emulsion or glaze can be used for this technique, although glaze will create a
far more translucent finish which is often more appealing. As the name of this
technique suggests, the sponge is actually used to apply the glaze to the wall.

1 Pour a little glaze onto an old
paint tub lid. Dip the sponge into
the glaze and remove any excess on
the rim of the lid or on a piece of
scrap paper.

2 Make a number of impressions
on the wall before reloading the
sponge with more glaze. Alter the
angle of the sponge slightly with each
new impression.

3 Reload the sponge and begin to
fill in the bare areas of wall,
gradually building up an even
coverage across the wall surface.

4 Once one colour is complete, use
a second colour to build up
depth in the design.

# SPONGING OFF

This technique differs slightly from sponging on in that the glaze is applied directly to the wall first and then a sponge is used to create impressions in the glazed surface. The finish tends to be slightly more subtle than sponging on, but equally effective in producing depth and texture.

1 Use a brush to apply the glaze to the wall, making brush strokes in random directions and taking care to ensure even coverage. Only cover an area of up to 1 sq m (1 sq yd) at a time, otherwise the glaze will start to dry in some places before you have the chance to produce the effect.

2 Press a dampened sponge into the glazed surface, creating a mottled broken-colour effect. As with sponging on, keep changing the angle at which the sponge comes into contact with the wall, to give a random, but even, finish.

3

REFLECTING TEXTURE
A sponged-off finish produces a wonderful overall effect that changes according to the intensity of light in which it is seen.

## SPONGING IDEAS

In addition to the standard sponging instructions, the following ideas can be added to the general technique.

- Using different sides: most natural sponges have one side that has a much finer texture than the other. Choose whichever side creates the effect you want, or combine both.
- Creating shadows: vary the intensity of the pattern by making more

impressions near any corners or alcoves – this will produce a very interesting shadowy effect.

- Dealing with corners: cut a small section off a sponge, tape it to the end of a pencil and use this to gain access to internal corners.
- Keeping clean: while working on this effect, wash the sponge frequently in plenty of clean water.

# RAGGING AND RAG-ROLLING

R ags, or to be more precise cotton cloths, are used in a similar way to sponges to create impressions on the wall surface with glaze. Although the technique is similar, the finished effect is quite different.

## RAGGING ON

Ragging on is similar to sponging on in that the rag is used to apply the glaze to the wall. You need to have a plentiful supply of rags to hand as they soon become too ingrained with glaze to be used effectively.

1 Pour some glaze onto an old plate or paint tub lid. Crumple the rag in your hand and dip it into the glaze. Remove any excess on the rim of the lid or on a scrap of paper.

2 In a similar fashion to sponging, press the rag onto the wall to create rag impressions. Keep altering the angle at which you apply the rag in order to create a random effect.

## RAGGING OFF

Ragging off is used here to create a textured impression in wet glaze. Only apply glaze to areas of up to 1 sq m (1 sq yd) – it has a limited workable time.

1 Apply the glaze randomly. For a more even finish, lay off the glaze (see page 32) in a vertical direction.

2 Press a damp, crumpled rag into the wet glaze, moving across it in a random manner.

# RAG-ROLLING

Rag-rolling extends the principle of using rags by making the impressions that they create much more directional. Rag-rolling can be carried out in any direction but by far the most common method is to use the rags to create vertical, relatively uniform striped patterns. Rag-rolling is much more effective using the 'ragging off' method, rather than the 'ragging on' one.

1 Screw up a number of pieces of rag and twist each one into an irregular sausage or finger shape. Make all the sausage shapes roughly the same size.

2 Apply the glaze to the wall then roll a sausage-shaped rag down the wall surface, creating a tumbling, relatively uniform ragged effect. Make sure that you keep the rag in contact with the wall surface at all times, using a continuous rolling motion to allow it to progress down the wall. Use a washed-out rag for each subsequent roll down the wall.

**3**

## RAGGING VARIATIONS

The name 'ragging' is used as an all-encompassing term when referring to the technique demonstrated above. In reality, rags or cotton cloths are not the only fabrics that can be used to create this paint effect. Try experimenting with any of the items in the following list – each one creates a slightly different, quite distinctive variation on the traditional ragged effect:

- plastic bags
- muslin
- denim
- netting
- hessian sacking
- velvet
- lace
- corduroy

THE FABRIC LOOK
Rag-rolling produces a highly textured fabric look on any wall surface. Although relatively simple to create, it gives the appearance of being extremely complicated.

# DRAGGING AND GRAINING

D ragging and graining are both effects that are used to produce a highly textured and directional finish. They can either be applied on a wooden surface to accentuate its texture, or on other surfaces to mimic the grain of wood. Both techniques require practice but, once mastered, the effects you can produce are extremely gratifying.

## DRAGGING

Dragging is a good effect to apply to any woodwork – especially panel doors. Specialist dragging brushes can be used although good effects can be created with a flogger or softening brush, or even a paintbrush with coarse bristles.

1 Apply the glaze to the door, treating different sections of the door as separate items.

2 Drag the brush through the glaze in the direction of the natural grain of the wood. Make sure that the bristles are at a very acute angle with the surface of the door. The coarseness in texture can be varied with the bristle angle.

3 After each sweep with the brush, remove excess glaze from the bristles with a clean cotton cloth.

4 Treat each section of the door as a separate item, creating precise dividing lines between each one.

3

# GRAINING

Graining bears some similarities to dragging, except that a specially designed tool – a graining rocker – must be used to create the desired effect. Graining can be carried out on wooden surfaces or, as in this case, the lower level of a wall can be grained to reproduce a wooden-panel effect.

1 Apply the glaze to the wall surface, taking care to lay off with vertical strokes of the brush.

2 Starting on the extreme edge of the wall, hold or fix a wooden batten so that it is precisely vertical. Then pull the graining rocker down through the glaze, using the edge of the batten as a guide.

3 The rest of the rocker strokes must now be made by eye – the wooden batten would damage the effect as you move across the surface. Make slight rolling motions with the rocker as you drag it through the wet glaze. This technique has the effect of mimicking the wooden knots and variations found in wood grain on the wall surface.

THE PANEL EFFECT

Graining is an extremely effective way of producing a mock panelled look on an otherwise flat, characterless wall surface.

# COLOURWASHING AND LIMING

Both these effects are aimed at highlighting the features of the base surface below. Whether on walls or wood, the idea is to produce a translucent finish that accentuates features in that surface by the use of colour and/or glaze.

## COLOURWASHING

A colourwash uses glaze to create a translucent layer over a base coat of emulsion or undercoat. Matt emulsion provides an absorbent base that soaks up the colourwash; a vinyl base coat will produce a more subtle look.

Wiping away: the wash is brushed on and immediately wiped away. This creates a translucent finish with varying degrees of colour intensity.

Leaving alone: alternatively, the wash can be applied with random brush strokes and left as the finished effect, creating a colour-dominant finish.

## TIMBER RUBBING

Timber rubbing can be considered as colourwashing on wood. The wood should have no base coat – glaze is applied directly to the untreated surface.

1 As with dragging, treat separate areas of the door as separate items, applying the glaze generously.

2 Use a damp rag to wipe away excess glaze to highlight the grain of the wood with a little glaze colour.

# LIMING

Liming creates a similar-looking effect to timber rubbing, except that white is the characteristic colour produced with the finish and the actual product used to create the finish is a purpose-designed wax rather than a glaze. It is essential that the wood is untreated before this effect is applied.

1 Open up the grain of the wood by scrubbing it lightly with a wire brush, working in the direction of the grain.

2 Apply generous amounts of the liming wax to the wooden surface using a ball of fine grade steel wool. Make sure that the wax gets into all areas.

3 Wipe off the excess wax with a cotton cloth. It is possible to buff up the surface giving it a slight sheen, characteristic of all waxed surfaces.

### THE LIMED LOOK
Liming produces a very traditional rustic finish on wood, and limed panelling such as this creates a very restful, comfortable atmosphere. Liming is especially effective when it is combined with natural materials and other aged or distressed paint effects in a room.

# MARBLING

**M**arbling is one of the most difficult paint effects to master: you are trying to reproduce the look of a natural substance. It takes a great deal of practice to achieve a really good marble effect, but it is possible to create this most luxurious-looking of all paint finishes. Marble differs hugely in colour and appearance; the marbling method shown here provides an attractive two-colour marble effect for the walls in your home.

1 Paint the wall with a white vinyl base coat; allow it to dry. Mix a light grey glaze and a raw umber glaze. Apply random patches of each glaze with a flat-bristled fitch; leave some areas of white uncovered.

2 While both the glazes are still wet, use a stippling brush across the entire wall surface to apply a textured effect and blend the two glazes into each other.

3 Use a softening brush or flogger to stroke gently across the glaze, blending both glazes still further and taking some of the harshness out of the stippled effect. First brush in the direction of the glaze, then across its grain, and then with the flow again.

4 Dip an artist's brush into some neat raw umber colourizer and then into each of the two glazes. Draw the brush across the surface of the wall while slowly rotating it between thumb and index finger. Keep the veins running in one direction to mimic natural marble.

**5** Soften the veins by first brushing in the direction they are running, then across their 'grain', and finally with their direction again.

**6** Allow the wall to dry completely before applying two to three coats of lacquer.

**7** Use a fine-grade abrasive paper to sand gently over the entire surface. Finally, polish up the finish using a soft cotton cloth.

3

**LUXURY FINISH**
A marbled paint effect is a luxurious finish in its own right – it also makes the wall a dramatic backdrop for ornaments and other display items.

# AGEING

There are many different ways of ageing a decorated surface in order to produce the comfortable, lived-in feel of years of wear and tear. The methods shown here are not the only ones, but they are extremely effective ways of creating this particular look.

## DISTRESSING

This technique is particularly effective on wooden panelled surfaces, as a large area displays the finish to best effect. Choose colours carefully when creating a distressed look – it always works best if you have a base colour that is a lighter shade than the top coat.

1 Apply the light base coat directly onto the untreated wood surface, and allow it to dry.

2 Where you want the colour to show through the top surface, apply random streaks of petroleum jelly, paying particular attention to the edges of the boards with just the odd streak along their central areas.

3 Apply the darker top coat over the entire panelled surface, taking care to cover it totally. Allow the top coat to dry.

4 Sand the panels with fine-grade abrasive paper. Where petroleum jelly was applied, the top coat will not stick; it rubs away to reveal the base colour. The degree of distressing depends on the amount of sanding.

# CRACKLE GLAZE

There are a number of different crackle finishes, but crackle glaze is one of the most effective ways of producing this aged, antique look. Application methods vary slightly between manufacturers, but the method shown here demonstrates the most commonly used technique for producing a crackle glaze finish.

1 Apply a base coat to the wall surface. Vivid, bright colours work particularly well with this effect; even the base coat should be a strong colour, so it shows up the finish as clearly as possible.

2 Apply the crackle glaze with a generously loaded brush. It is essential to keep the brush strokes going in the same direction.

3 Thin the top coat of emulsion with one part water to 10 parts paint. Apply it using brush strokes at right angles to each other, never crossing each other. Don't return to an area once it has been painted. Slowly the crackle effect will appear.

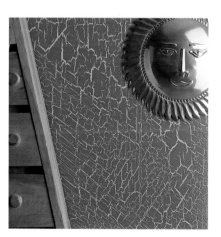

NATURAL CRACKLE
Crackle glaze produces a fascinating, crazed effect, combining both colour and texture to great effect.

# STIPPLING

S tippling produces a fine, textured effect across a wall, and it can be built up in layers to produce greater depth. Flat open surfaces are best suited to stippling as they maintain consistency of texture.

1 Apply the glaze to the wall with slightly swirling brush strokes, in all directions. Total coverage is not necessary, as small patches of base coat will be covered with glaze once stippling begins.

2 Once an area of 1 sq m (1 sq yd) has been covered with glaze, use the stippling brush to make small impressions in the surface. Make short dabbing motions, allowing only the very tips of the bristles to come in contact with the wall. Vary your hand angle as you gradually progress across the wall. Once one area is complete, apply more glaze to the wall and continue to stipple as before. Remove excess glaze from the bristles with a clean cotton cloth after each glazed area is complete.

3 Use a stencil brush to complete the effect in the corner junction – it is difficult to gain access to internal corners with a stippling brush.

STIPPLING EFFECT
Stippling creates a wonderful, warm glow across a wall surface. Light is refracted with different intensities, producing a truly three-dimensional finish.

# COMBING

A special tool called a graining comb is used on a stippled surface to create this highly textured, decorative effect. Graining combs vary in design, but all produce a directional flow of glaze that combines the base and glaze colour to produce a two-tone effect. The comb shown here has differing gaps and sizes of teeth that can be used to create different grades of effect.

1 Apply glaze in random directions across the wall surface in areas of up to 1 sq m (1 sq yd) at a time, as the glaze has a limited workable time before it dries. Take care to cover the area totally.

2 For a more even effect, stipple the glaze to give a uniform, textured finish. See opposite for the technique of using a stippling brush.

3 Draw the comb down through the glaze to create a grooved effect, removing any excess glaze from the teeth of the comb with a dry cloth after each sweep.

VARYING TEXTURE
By combining two sizes of comb, it is possible to create an interesting striped effect such as this one.

# STAMPING

S tamping is a quick and easy way of applying and repeating painted images across a wall or wooden surface. The images can be applied singly or in groups, and may be used to create single-feature designs or mixed with other stamps to produce a collage effect. Stamps can either be bought or made – the application method remains the same.

## HOUSEHOLD OBJECTS

Stamps can be made out of any number of objects found around the home, as long as the item chosen can absorb paint. A small brush can be used to apply paint to a stamp, or you can use a custom-made roller as shown opposite.

**3**

Sponges: draw an animal design on a sponge and cut it out using a craft knife. Reloading the sponge after each stamp is not necessary because it is so absorbent.

Corks: bind three corks together with sticky tape to create a clover leaf design. Reload the corks with paint after each stamp. Make the stem of the leaf with a small fitch or by rotating the painted edge of a single cork below the clover design.

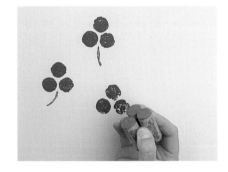

Potatoes: cut a potato in half and draw a picture on one half. Cut out the design with a craft knife. Make sure that the entire surface area of the design is placed in contact with the wall before removing it to reveal the impression.

## CUSTOM-MADE STAMPS

Although making your own stamps is great fun, manufactured stamps tend to be easier to use and create far more defined impressions when applied to the wall. Choose a design that fits in with the particular theme and effect you are trying to create in your room.

1 Load up a small foam roller with the chosen paint colour. Apply it to the stamp, ensuring that the entire design is covered. Before applying it to the wall, test the stamp on a piece of scrap paper to check whether you need to remove excess paint from its face before applying it to the wall.

2 Apply the stamp to the wall, making sure that there is total contact between the design and wall surface. Press down firmly.

3 Pull the stamp away from the wall, taking care not to smudge the design, and continue to apply further stamps to build up your overall picture. Reload the stamp with paint as required.

CREATING A THEME
Stamps are ideal for creating a decorative theme in a room – they can be used to make a subtle design or a more dramatic effect.

# STRAIGHTFORWARD STENCILLING

S tencils are similar to stamps in that they provide a technique for producing a design on a wall or wooden surface. However, the way in which stencils achieve this effect is completely different from the method for stamping. Stencils can be bought or made – making your own gives greater opportunity for personal expression and effect.

## MAKING A STENCIL

Stencils can be made out of custom-made card or acetate. Acetate tends to be the most practical choice, as it is easily washed and can be used time and time again with equal accuracy. Stencil designs can either be drawn by hand or traced, and you can use various natural products as the basis for your design.

1   Choose a leaf cluster that demonstrates a strong shape as well as balanced overall design. Place it on a board, using some sticky tape to hold it in place if required. Hold some tracing paper over the top of it and use a pencil to trace around the edge of the leaves.

3   Remove the tracing paper and stick the acetate onto the board with masking tape. Follow the felt-tip guideline to cut out the leaves, stem and stalk of the design, using a sharp craft knife. The stencil is then ready to use.

2   Remove the leaves, and stick the traced image onto the board with some masking tape. Hold a sheet of acetate over the tracing paper, and use a felt-tip pen to draw the traced design onto the acetate.

# USING A STENCIL

The design below can be used as a border around doors or windows, or as a more overall wall pattern as demonstrated here. Custom-made acrylic stencil paints are the ideal materials to use for filling in the design. For a more imaginative finish, try mixing colour with emulsion and colourizers.

1 Use some masking tape to hold the stencil securely in position on the wall surface.

2 When using a stencil brush, load the brush with paint so that the bristles remain relatively dry – the excess paint can be removed by dabbing the brush a few times on a scrap piece of paper to leave just a trace of colour on the brush. Brush on the colour, using light dabbing motions perpendicular to the wall surface. Vary the colour within the design to make it look lifelike.

3 Once complete, remove the stencil carefully to reveal the finished design. Move along to the next area and repeat steps 1 and 2.

COLOURFUL STENCILLING
Stencils can produce well-defined images on all manner of surfaces, such as walls, mirrors and furniture. Single motifs can be used, as here, to cover all or part of the area that you wish to decorate.

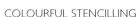

# CREATING STENCIL EFFECTS

As your technique improves, it is possible to create more specialist effects with stencils. The increased use of colour, shading different areas with more paint, or highlighting parts of a stencil more than others, can create a shadow effect that hints at the light direction and produces a more three-dimensional appearance. Shading more on one side of a stencil gives the effect of direct sunlight and indicates the direction from which it is coming. Alternatively, making the edges of a flower design more pronounced, as shown here, gives a very vibrant, lifelike finish to the stencil.

1

2

1 Attach the stencil to the wall with masking tape. Increase the colour intensity on the extreme edges of the design, while leaving central areas more sparsely coloured.

2 Carefully remove the stencil to reveal a textured effect that demonstrates more depth than the more simple stencil techniques.

## ALTERNATIVE STENCILLING MATERIALS

In addition to standard stencil brushes, it is possible to use various other tools to apply paint to a stencil.
- Sponges: natural sea sponges have a pronounced texture that makes them ideal for use on large stencils; always remove excess paint before applying the sponge.
- Aerosols: as the spray cannot be pinpointed on a small area, aerosol

paints are best used for stencil designs that do not require close colour changes. They are very quick to use.
- Crayons: stencil crayons are a good alternative to traditional paints. The sticks can be rubbed on a piece of acetate that can then be used as a palette for transferring the colour to the stencil with a stencil brush.

# PAPERING TECHNIQUES

*Wallpaper varies in design, pattern and size, but the actual technique for applying the different types changes very little. Once you have established a sound, basic papering technique, you can hang nearly all types of paper with equal success. This chapter outlines the simple rules and correct techniques for tackling straightforward wallpapering. Once this stage is mastered, it is simply a matter of refining these techniques for more complicated wallpapering situations. Follow all the necessary preparations outlined in Chapter 1 before beginning to hang the wallpaper, and don't try to hurry the papering process – speed will develop with experience and in the initial stages may cause you to make mistakes.*

4

# WHAT PAPER TO USE WHERE

**M**ost paper can be applied in any area of the home, although some types of wallpaper are more suited to particular rooms than others (see page 15 for the properties of each type of paper). However, it is worth considering the effects of different designs and patterns in conjunction with the use of the room and the style you are trying to achieve.

**The formal choice:** dining rooms and reception areas are the ideal places to use traditional designs, which can be linked to the period of the property or simply to add a touch of grandeur and style to the room as a whole.

**Practical papering:** in kitchens and bathrooms, use vinyl papers, so that the wall surfaces can be wiped down and cleaned very easily. A striped design, such as this one, produces a precise, elegant look which is suited to most areas in the home.

**Having fun:** children's rooms offer the chance to choose fun designs to create a happy, playful atmosphere.

4

## THE EFFECTS OF DESIGN

Different designs on wallpapers can create completely different effects. In much the same way as colour can produce a particular feeling within a room, the pattern of the wallpaper can completely alter the atmosphere and mood; when choosing a design always take into consideration the effect that the design in question will have on the room as a whole.

### Stripes
Striped wallpapers always create a feeling of height and are, therefore, ideal for rooms in which you want to give the impression of 'raising' the ceiling. Don't use striped wallpaper on uneven walls, as any slight undulations will be accentuated by the clear, sharp lines of the stripes.

### All-over effects
Recent fashion has meant that there are a number of papers on the market that have an all-over, almost paint effect design, such as a colourwash or stippled effect. These wallpapers tend to be easy to hang, but it can be quite difficult to hide joins as there is no precise pattern to draw your eye away from them. This happens with darker colours in particular, and it is worth thinking about painting the lining paper a similar base colour to the wallpaper, so that any slightly open seams will on the wallpaper will have the appropriate background colour.

### Floral papers
These are generally easy to hang as they tend to have a fairly busy design that hides the joins easily. Big floral patterns should be hung in large rooms, otherwise the pattern can look cramped and make the room seem smaller than it actually is. Small floral patterns tend to create a country cottage effect and they are ideal for uneven or slightly rough walls because the busy pattern on the paper draws your eye away from any imperfections in the wall surface.

### Singular designs
Wallpapers with one or two motifs that repeat need to be matched precisely – if the paper is not hung exactly vertical, any discrepancies will be very obvious on the wall. While they produce an excellent effect, these papers are not the easiest ones for a beginner to hang.

### Papered scenes
Some manufacturers produce papers with landscape designs. The rolls of paper have to be applied to the wall surface in a particular sequence in order to build up a precise picture. This unusual effect can produce an impressive finish in any room as long as the size of the design can be fitted into the available wall space. Similar to these papers are *trompe-l'œil* paper panels, which can be used to create another *faux* effect on a wallpapered surface in a room.

### Period papers
Some paper designs have a classical appeal that never seems to go out of fashion or age over the generations – the fleur-de-lys design, for example, has been copied for many years and still maintains its popular appeal. Many of these classic designs produce quite a formal decorative effect in a room and this factor should always be taken into consideration when choosing this type of wallpaper.

4

# MEASURING, CUTTING AND PASTING

E nsuring that you have the right number of rolls for the job is obviously an important factor when papering. The way in which these rolls are prepared, cut and pasted, ready for applying to the wall, is also essential in producing the right finish. Whatever type of wallpaper is being used, the dimensions of the room must be measured accurately.

## CALCULATING THE NUMBER OF ROLLS

A simple way of calculating the number of rolls required for a room is shown below. Manufacturers usually state the size of the pattern repeat on the roll label, but it is worth checking it yourself.

$$\frac{\text{Height of room} + \text{Wallpaper repeat size} \times \text{Distance around skirting}}{\text{Area of one roll}} = \frac{\text{Number of}}{\text{rolls required}}$$

### AREA OF ONE ROLL

Most wallpapers are about 10 m (11 yd) long by 52 cm (20½ in) wide. However, there are variations, so work out the surface area of one roll of paper by multiplying the two dimensions together.

Adjust your calculations if entire walls are taken up by picture windows or fitted units. However, doors and other smaller areas that do not need wallpapering should be included, as you will need to make allowances for trimming the paper while fitting around them.

**4**

## MEASURING TO CUT

Measuring wallpaper to fit is a simple process as long as a few simple rules are followed. First, measure the height of a required length by measuring the exact distance between the ceiling to the top of the skirting board. Next, the size of the pattern repeat must be added to this measurement and, finally, an extra 2.5 cm (1 in) must be added at the top and bottom of the length to account for trimming. With particularly large repeats, this method can produce a lot of wastage. It is often better to hold up a roll of dry wallpaper next to the previously hung length and match it, so that it can be cut precisely and then pasted before it is applied to the wall. For patterns with no repeat, such as stripes, only the allowance for trimming need be added to the standard height measurement. This means that with patterns that have little or no repeat, it is easier to cut a number of lengths in readiness for hanging, whereas with larger repeat patterns, it is often easier to cut one length to size at a time.

# PASTING PAPER

Wallpapers are divided into two categories: ready-pasted paper with dry paste attached to its backing, which is reactivated by submerging in cold water, and unpasted paper, which requires traditional paste to stick it onto the wall.

## READY-PASTED PAPER

1 Two-thirds fill a water trough on the floor at the end of the pasting table. Roll up a length of wallpaper, pattern inwards, and submerge it for the recommended soaking time.

2 Pull the paper onto the table, folding so that pasted surface meets pasted surface. Repeat this step at the other end of the length. Leave it to soak for the required time.

## UNPASTED PAPER

1 Roll out the wallpaper along the pasting table. Make sure that the paste is mixed according to the manufacturer's instructions for the type of paper that you are using. Apply the paste from the centre of the paper out towards its edges, ensuring total and even coverage.

2 When the paper is covered with paste, pick up the end of the length and lift and slide it along the pasting table, folding it into a concertina design as you progress along the whole length of it.

3 Remove the folded length of paper from the pasting table and allow the paste to soak into the paper for the required time specified by the manufacturer before applying it to the wall.

# LINING

L ining paper is applied to the walls in order to create the best possible surface for the wallpaper. It acts in a similar way to an undercoat before the top coat of paint. Although it is not essential, a lining paper greatly improves a wallpapered finish and, in many cases, manufacturer's guidelines state that lining is vital before applying their wallpaper. Paste is applied to lining paper in the same way as for wallpaper (see page 69).

## CEILINGS

Although ceilings are not often wallpapered, they can benefit from being lined. Whether lining a ceiling for wallpapering or painting, make sure that the surface is thoroughly prepared before applying the lining paper, and check that the correct sealer or size has been applied.

Using the wall/ceiling junction as the starting point, begin lining. Alternatively, begin in the centre of the room in order to bisect the pendant light fitting (see opposite).

Support the paper with one hand while brushing out with other hand.

Start near the natural light source and line away from it in order to make any joins less visible.

Use planks to create a sturdy platform to walk along.

Use trestles or stepladders as supports for the platform.

Allow the lining paper to run onto the platform surface, ensuring that the pasted side is facing up.

4

# HANGING GUIDELINES

Ceilings may appear awkward to paper, but they can be easier than walls as they have far fewer obstacles. Beginning each length from a secure starting point is essential if you are to paper your ceiling successfully.

1 Brush the start of the length securely into the ceiling/wall junction, allowing a small overlap for trimming. Progress along the length, brushing out air bubbles and joining each length precisely to each other.

2 At each wall/ceiling junction, pull back the wallpaper and cut along the creased guideline. To make the guideline more visible, you can mark the crease with a pencil before pulling the paper back.

3 Brush the trimmed paper back into position, to create a perfect cut edge.

# DEALING WITH LIGHT FITTINGS

Pendant light fittings can be dealt with in two different ways, as shown below. Whenever papering around electrical fittings, ensure that the power is turned off at the consumer unit before work commences.

Coinciding seams: if the paper will bisect the pendant, loosen its backing plate and brush the paper behind it.

Threading: cut a hole in the paper and thread pendant through. Cut strips to mould around pendant; trim strips.

# LINING WALLS

Traditionally, lining paper is applied to walls horizontally, although this is not essential. It is best to apply lining paper so that the minimum number of lengths are used on any particular wall, whether this is vertically or horizontally. This means that large walls are best lined horizontally and small alcoves are best lined vertically. When lining vertically, you must always make sure that when it comes to wallpapering, the lining-paper seams and the wallpaper seams do not coincide. The examples below show how to line walls horizontally; the vertical method can be achieved using the wallpapering guidelines shown later in the chapter.

**4**

1 Join lengths of paper at the corner junction, allowing for a small overlap for trimming purposes. Hold the paper concertina in one hand while positioning with the other hand.

2 Using a paper-hanging brush, smooth out the length, gradually unrolling the concertina and joining the paper with the previous length. Always butt-join the lengths and avoid any overlaps.

3 Trim the paper into the corners, using scissors or a craft knife, as shown here.

## CORNERS

For internal corners, the lining paper should always be trimmed along the corner junction, as shown opposite. External corners require the paper to be moulded around the edge of the corner in order to maintain the continuity of a single length. The method demonstrated here will only work if the external corner is square. Where this is not the case, it may be necessary to use the method for dealing with external corners when wallpapering (see page 82).

1 Unroll the concertina, allowing the paper to bend around the edge of the external corner and onto the adjacent wall.

2 Before brushing the paper out on the adjacent wall, use your fingers to crease along the edge of the corner, smoothing out and removing any air bubbles.

## FINISHING OFF

Once the room is lined and the paper has dried, fill any gaps with filler (see below) to make a perfectly smooth surface for wallpapering. Apply some 'size' (dilute wallpaper paste) to the lining paper and allow it to dry – this will make it much easier to hang the wallpaper because it allows the paper to slip across the lined surface when you are positioning it.

4

Filling gaps: if there are gaps between joins in the lined surface, apply some fine filler to these areas to make a smooth surface. Sand the area lightly once the filler is dry.

Finishing corners: decorator's caulk around all the internal corner junctions and joints between lining paper and wood provides an even finish and stops the paper lifting.

# WHERE TO START WALLPAPERING

T here are a number of factors to consider when deciding on the best place to begin wallpapering. In order to make sure that the wallpaper will create the best possible effect, you need to take a little time to decide on the most appropriate starting point as well as the best place to finish and join up the pattern as a whole. As room designs and layouts vary dramatically, it is difficult to cover every eventuality here. However, there are a number of points that can be considered as general guidelines when deciding where to begin.

**Centralizing:** bold patterned papers with large repeats may require the main design in the paper to be centralized on a particular wall in order to create a balanced overall effect. The obvious place would be on a chimney breast or centrally between two windows on the same wall. With smaller patterns, this process is not as essential as the balance of the design will not be dependent on central positioning.

**A complete start:** always try to make sure that the first length you hang is a complete uninterrupted hang that requires no intricate trimming. Never trust an internal corner as a vertical starting point – it is best to use a spirit level to ensure that you are starting from a precisely vertical position.

**Avoiding the join:** where a room does not have a continuous wall surface around the entire circumference of the room, avoid having to join the paper at the end of the job. This avoids the need for what can often be a tricky pattern match in order to finish the room.

**4**

**Marking the position:** work out where subsequent lengths of paper will hang by measuring around the circumference of the room with a roll of wallpaper. Mark off positions on the wall and adjust accordingly for the most suitable positions for lengths to hang.

# THE STARTING POINTS

### Centralizing

Finish here.          First length.

After the first length, paper around this corner of the chimney-breast.

Continue around the other corner of the chimney-breast and on around the rest of the room.

### A complete start

After the first length, continue around the rest of the room.

Final length may need to overlap in the corner to create a join.

Finish here.     First length.

**4**

### Avoiding the join

First length.

Finish here.

After the first length, continue around the rest of the room.

# HANGING THE FIRST LENGTH

H anging the first length correctly is the most important part of creating any wallpaper design, as this initial application forms the base on which the rest of the pattern is built. If the first length is not vertical, this will be repeated throughout the entire room so it is vital to take time to make sure that the first length is straight.

**4**

1 At your starting position, draw a pencil line from ceiling to floor, using a spirit level to ensure that it is precisely vertical.

2 Position the first length at the top of the wall, and slide it into place so the edge of the paper runs along the pencil guideline. Allow a small overlap onto the ceiling.

3 Crease the top of the paper into the wall/ceiling junction then work down the paper with a paper-hanging brush to remove air bubbles and ensure that the paper is firmly stuck to the wall. Work the bristles of the brush from the centre of the length outwards and downwards.

4 When you reach the bottom of the length, use the paper-hanging brush to crease the paper securely into the skirting-board junction.

5 Return to the top of the length then cut along the wall/ceiling junction with a craft knife. Cut slightly above the junction as this tends to give a far neater finish.

6 Brush back down to the bottom of the length and trim the paper with a craft knife, cutting slightly onto the top of the skirting board to produce a clean dividing line.

7 Return to the top of the length then brush all the way down to the bottom again, removing any air bubbles that may have been missed during the initial sweep.

8 Finally, use a sponge rinsed in clean water to wipe over the surface of the entire length of paper to remove any paste residue. Wipe over the adjacent areas of wall and skirting board as well, to ensure that they are paste-free.

# JOINING LENGTHS

W hether a wallpaper has a pattern that requires matching or not, adjacent lengths of paper need to be joined very accurately to produce a good finish. The aim should be to butt-join the lengths so that the two pieces form a seam where they meet, without overlapping.

## MAKING THE JOIN

Where the pattern requires precise matching, it is obviously important to make the match between papers as precise as possible. However, some papers are prone to stretching, and some may even have slight variations within a roll, which makes it difficult to match the pattern. Always try to make the first point of joining at normal eye level in the room; if there are cases where the pattern drops, these inconsistencies will be positioned lower down the wall where they will be far less visible.

1 Slide the new length up to the previous one, matching the pattern first at eye level, and then down the rest of the length. Brush out and trim the length in the usual way.

2 Most papers will join easily, but it may be necessary to run a seam roller lightly down the joints to ensure a good finish.

3 Where the edges dry out too quickly, apply some more paste with a fitch, then stick the paper down again as required.

# TYPES OF MATCH

Wallpaper patterns are matched between lengths using more than one method. It is important to be aware of the subtle differences between the designs as these can affect the way in which pattern matching is achieved. Use the best method for the particular paper you are trying to hang.

Straight match: the join for a straight-match pattern is made very simple by having the match bisect a main feature in the design itself – when two pieces of paper are being joined, it is perfectly clear where the second paper should be positioned in order to reunite the pattern.

## MISCELLANEOUS MATCHES

Some designers produce papers that vary from the matches shown here – in such cases, instructions are usually supplied with the paper. Sometimes, a straight-match paper design is slightly 'offset' so that joining lengths is not as clear as in most cases. Also, some free-match papers are, in fact, straight match, which may only become apparent once the paper is hung. Always read the manufacturer's guidelines before hanging a wallpaper, especially when the design is not straightforward.

**4**

Free match: these are often the easiest papers to join as you don't need to worry about matching the pattern at specific points – it is butt-joined at any point. However, manufacturers often suggest that for papers with a strong overall pattern, every second length should be inverted.

Level match: with some wallpapers the actual match is free, but the paper design of each length needs to be level with the previous one. Once a length has been applied, use a spirit level to check that the whole design remains constant and in the correct position on the wall.

# INTERNAL CORNERS

A s all rooms have internal corners, learning how to deal with them is an important part of basic papering technique. However square an internal corner is, never try to bend a full length of paper around it because the paper will always wrinkle along the junction, producing an unsightly finish. The best technique is to cut a single length in two and rejoin it precisely along the corner junction.

1 Measure the exact distance from the last full length to the corner junction. Check this distance along the entire length to make sure there are no slight variations along the junction. Add 12 mm (½ in) to this measurement, and cut the next length of paper into two pieces accordingly.

2 Paste up the first length, and pattern-match it as usual to the previous length.

3 Brush it into place, allowing for the 12 mm (½ in) overlap to bend round onto the adjacent wall.

4 Paste the other half of the length of paper and position it on the adjacent wall, matching the pattern as well as possible. Undulations along the corner junction may mean that the match is not exact in some places. However, the length must be hung vertically, so use a spirit level to make sure that it hangs in the correct position on the wall.

5 Make sure that the edge of the second half of the length is well stuck down, especially along the corner junction. Trim off any excess paper as required.

4

6 Use a clean dampened sponge to wipe away any excess paste from both the surface of the wallpaper and also from the ceiling and the skirting board respectively.

7 To ensure that the corner stays stuck down – especially vinyl paper – pull back the edge and apply overlap adhesive along the junction. Push the paper back into position.

# EXTERNAL CORNERS

T he technique for dealing with external corners varies considerably from the one for internal corners. Where these corners are square, it is possible to bend wallpaper around them and continue along the wall as normal. However, in most cases, a length will cease to be level as it rounds the corner, and an alternative technique is required.

1 Bend the wallpaper around the corner and trim to fit as well as possible. Take care not to allow the paper to tear at ceiling or skirting board level.

2 Apply a second length of paper, overlapping the first, matching the pattern on the overlap close to the corner. Trim the length top and bottom to fit.

3 Hold a level vertically in the centre of the overlapping lengths, and cut through both pieces of paper using a craft knife. Continue the cut from ceiling to skirting.

4 Peel back the second length of paper and then remove the two excess strips of wallpaper that have been produced by the cut with the craft knife.

5 Smooth back the second length of paper to produce a perfect butt-join. It may be necessary to use a seam roller along the length of the join to produce a perfect flat match.

6 This technique is quite messy and results in a lot of paste getting onto the wallpaper surface. Be sure to remove all of this residue with a clean, damp sponge.

## EXTERNAL CORNER CONSIDERATIONS

- Cutting: the most important thing to consider is where to create the overlap before cutting through the lengths. This will depend on how far the first length of paper bends around the corner and the most appropriate place to match the pattern. For papers with an open background, it is best to cut through the background rather than the main part of the pattern. For wallpapers with a more complicated or busy design, it is less important where you overlap and cut.

- Keeping level: when matching the second length to the first one, there may need to be some compromise between exact pattern-matching and keeping the paper vertical. Ensuring that the paper is precisely vertical is the first priority; after that, join the pattern as accurately as possible, paying particular attention at eye level. Use a spirit level to make sure that the edge of the second length is vertical and can then act as a good starting point for papering the rest of the wall surface.

# PROBLEM SOLVING

**M**ost papering problems are due to poor application and general technique, though sometimes a particular paper can be difficult to hang. Whatever the reason, most problems can be overcome or any damage can be repaired – things that do require work to put right, represent a good lesson for future projects.

**4**

**Lifting seams:** in any room, it is likely that some seams will dry out and come away from the wall. Simply reapply some paste to the area and stick the paper down again; remove excess paste.

**White seams:** where dark colours are joined, the lining paper will show through if the seams do not match precisely. Use a felt-tip pen the same colour as the paper to touch-in these areas.

**Tearing:** wallpaper is vulnerable to tearing just after it has been applied, while it is still wet. Most tears look worse than they are; it should be possible to tease the paper back in place and stick it down.

**Shiny seams:** this is the result of overbrushing the seams during paper application and/or the presence of paste along the seam. Wash seams with a mild detergent and then rinse with clean water.

**Poor pattern match:** the paper may have stretched so that the pattern matches in some areas but not in others. Most small mistakes will not be noticeable, but take greater care in future.

**Bubbles:** bubbles occur when wallpaper has not been left for the correct soaking time before applying it. Small bubbles can be split open and stuck down. Large areas will need to be stripped and redone.

# PAPERING AWKWARD AREAS

*Having mastered the basic wallpapering technique, dealing with more complex obstacles on a wall surface becomes progressively easier and less daunting. Most obstacles require trimming around, and this tends to be the difficult part. The secret of wallpapering these areas is precise trimming, which, in effect, means taking a little extra time when there is a lot of intricate cutting and trimming involved. Creating clear, sharp edges and accurate joins will make the end product far more impressive. For those areas of the home that are an awkward shape, such as stairwells, taking your time is, again, the crucial factor. This way you can keep to the right order of work, which, in turn, will produce the best finish.*

5

# DOORS AND ENTRANCES

A ll rooms have a doorway of some description, so it is essential to know the best way of papering around them. Most doors have a frame or architrave, which makes papering much easier; however, some entrances have no doors or frames and these require a different technique altogether.

## DOORS

Always ignore the door itself and concentrate on the architrave because this has a precise edge to paper up to, which makes papering a straightforward exercise in cutting and trimming.

1 Allow the length of paper to flop loosely over the corner of the architrave, taking care not to tear the paper. Make a diagonal cut back to the corner.

2 Use the paper-hanging brush to crease the paper carefully into the architrave/wall junction both at the side and above the door.

3 Trim the excess paper with a craft knife, and remove residual paste from the paper and door frame with a damp sponge.

# ARCHES

An entrance that does not contain
a door or frame is more difficult
to paper around, especially if it is
a curved one, such as an arch.
However, as long as the correct
technique is followed, it is possible to
paper an archway very successfully.

Allow lengths of paper on the main wall to go
over and beyond the edge of the arch.

Trim the paper back to 2.5 cm (1 in) from
the edge of the arch.

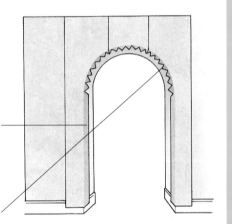

On the straight edges of the arch, bend the
paper around the edge, allowing it to stick
on the internal wall of the arch.

On the curved edges of the arch, make a
number of cuts in the paper at right angles
to the edge in order to bend the paper around
the edge. The small flaps can then be stuck
to the internal edge of the curve.

Cut two pieces of paper to run inside the arch.

Ensure a straight edge along the corner junction.

Join the two pieces at the top of the arch.

5

# WINDOWS

W indows that are not recessed into the wall, and therefore have no sill, can be treated in a similar manner to doors, since the wallpaper is simply trimmed up to the window frame or surround. However, where the window is recessed, the papering technique needs to be adjusted to take into account the edges and corners.

## RECESSED WINDOWS

Recessed windows, which are present in most homes, vary in shape and size, but the technique used to paper around them is the same, whatever the shape. Following the correct order of work and precise cutting is all that is required to overcome these obstacles.

1 Allow the wallpaper to overlap the reveal, making sure that it is also stuck firmly in position on the wall. Use scissors to make a horizontal cut back to the corner of the reveal precisely along the top edge of the reveal.

2 Make a similar horizontal cut along the bottom edge of the reveal, back to the corner of the window sill. It may be necessary to use a craft knife to cut around the corner of the sill to release the required flap of paper above.

3 Bend the flap of paper around the external corner of the reveal, creasing it into the frame-edge junction. Trim it with a craft knife to fit accurately.

4 Apply another length of paper overlapping the previous length. The second length should be just long enough for the bottom edge of it to reach around the top of the recess to the window frame when trimmed to fit. Match the pattern very carefully all along the overlap.

5 Use a craft knife and a straight edge (a spirit level is ideal) to cut diagonally through the area where the two pieces of wallpaper overlap, back to the reveal corner.

6 Use scissors to trim the bottom section of the second length back to the reveal corner and the diagonal cut made in step 5.

7 Peel back the second length of wallpaper and discard the excess paper below it (the top section of the first length).

8 Smooth the second length back to create a perfect butt-join with the first length. Fold the bottom part of the second length under the reveal, then trim to fit around the frame, as required. Finally, sponge off excess paste with a damp sponge. Continue along to the other end of the window and repeat the process around the other reveal.

# WALL SWITCHES AND SOCKETS

E lectrical wall sockets and switches are common obstacles in most rooms so it is important to know the most appropriate technique for wallpapering around them. The technique for wallpapering around switches and power points is the same. As with all electrical fittings, make sure that the power is turned off at the mains before you begin to work around them.

1 Allow the paper to hang over the front of the switch and carefully mould the paper to its outline, taking care not to make any tears or rips across the paper surface.

2 Make a pencil mark slightly in from each of the four corners.

3 Use scissors to cut four diagonal lines from the centre of the switch plate out to the marks. This creates four triangular flaps.

5

4 Carefully cut away each flap, thus making a square hole in the wallpaper, slightly smaller than the switch plate itself.

5 Loosen the retaining screws on the switch plate until it comes free from the wall surface.

6 By carefully moving the plate into a diagonal position, it is possible to pull it through the square in the wallpaper, allowing the cut edges of the wallpaper to be hidden behind the plate.

7 Tighten up the retaining screws, making sure that the switch plate is level. Use a dry cloth to remove any excess paste. Do not turn the electricity back on until the plate is totally dry.

5

# WALL OBSTACLES

**M**ost obstacles encountered along a wall surface can be overcome using the techniques already demonstrated, or by combining techniques. If at all possible, try and remove the obstacle.

## DEALING WITH RADIATORS

Radiators are an awkward shape to paper around and they require ingenuity and patience. Remember that the join behind a radiator will not be seen; the areas to concentrate on are those directly around and just behind the edge.

1 Allow the length of paper to hang loosely over the front of the radiator. Cut slits in the paper to correspond with the brackets that support the weight of the radiator.

2 Use a radiator roller to push the paper behind the radiator, positioning it so that the cut in the paper coincides with the position of the supporting bracket.

## RADIATOR REMOVAL

**5**

Radiators should only be removed if you have some plumbing experience. If a radiator is taken off, remove the brackets but replace screw fixings. Use the paper-hanging brush to smooth the paper over the screws, allowing them to pierce the paper. Unscrew the screws and re-attach the bracket; repeat with the next length.

# MISCELLANEOUS OBSTACLES

For all the other obstacles that may be encountered, common sense and planning are the best tools for successfully wallpapering around them. The guidelines below deal with some of the more common ones.

## COMMON OBSTACLES

- Lights: if possible, remove wall lights, paper the area and refit the lights. Remember to turn off the electricity before disconnecting the light.
- Hooks: it is always best to remove hooks before wallpapering unless you are certain that pictures will be hung back in the same place. A new pattern or design often leads to a different choice of picture, and starting afresh after wallpapering is usually the best policy.
- Phone sockets: these can be treated in the same way as electrical sockets (see page 90). Carefully undo the front plate from a phone socket then undo the retaining screws that fix it to the wall. Take care not to dislodge any wires when carrying out this procedure.
- Fireplaces: these are nothing more than intricate mouldings, the next stage on from papering around a door architrave. Make cuts in the paper at right angles to the fireplace profile then the paper will mould easily around its edge and make it easier to trim with a craft knife.
- Toilets: the cistern usually has a curved edge, which makes it difficult for you to trim around it accurately.

Take the top off the cistern, if possible, then apply the paper before replacing the top. This produces a very neat edge at this level. For the sides, trim the paper to slightly less than appears to be the correct size. The excess paper can then be pushed into the curved junction, creating a neat finish.

- Basins: these are similar to toilets. However, bear in mind that it is never sensible to wallpaper directly above a basin as water splashes will soon damage the paper; it is best to tile these areas.
- Wall cupboards: try and remove any wall cupboards before starting to paper, as trimming around them can be a difficult and time consuming job. Remember to mark fixing holes so the cupboards can be put back once papering is complete.
- Kitchen units: these can be treated in a similar way to wall cupboards as most kitchen wall units can be taken down and repositioned after papering. Floor units are generally permanently fixed. The area directly above work surfaces is better tiled; if it is wallpapered, the paper will deteriorate rapidly.

5

# STAIRWELLS

W orking in stairwells has the problem of access and safety. It is essential to construct a stable, safe platform so that you can reach all those areas that would otherwise be inaccessible. In addition, there are a number of other factors that you must take into consideration if you are going to make the best possible job of wallpapering a stairwell.

## STAIRWELL CONSIDERATIONS

- Types of pattern: stairwells are by nature tall and relatively thin, so consider what effect the pattern of your wallpaper will have on such an area. Stripes, for example, will make the stairwell appear even taller.
- Two people: the ideal set-up for papering a stairwell is to have one person positioning the paper at the top while a second person holds the paper away from the wall at the bottom. It can be done on your own but two people makes the job a lot easier.
- Using a level: when applying the first length in a stairwell, use a spirit level to check that the paper is vertical up and down the entire length. Long lengths have a tendency to swerve off level at the bottom even if they are totally vertical at the top.
- Wall bannister: try and remove any bannisters or rails from walls that are to be papered, otherwise they

will make the task much more fiddly. Fix them back on once the papering is complete.
- Adjust the platform: not all stairwell set-ups are like the one shown opposite. Where necessary, adjust platforms with extra ladders, steps and planks to account for turns in the staircase, or more complicated designs than a simple straight run of stairs.
- Soaking times: be accurate and consistent with the time you leave the wallpaper to soak after it has been pasted and before it goes on the wall. Fluctuating these times from length to length can cause pattern matching problems, which will be accentuated over the long joins in a stairwell.

5

# THE STAIRWELL SET-UP

Designs vary, but safety should always be the primary concern when building a platform in a stairwell. Make sure that all the equipment you are using is in good condition and able to withstand the stresses that will be put upon it.

Position of first hang – work away from this length both at the top and lower level of the stairs.

Use rope to bind the plank to the ladder and stepladder.

Paper once side walls are finished.

Use padding on top of the ladder to protect the wall surface.

Depending on the length and thickness of the plank that is used, more support may be needed here.

5

# BORDERS

B orders add a decorative edge to a wall finish. They can either be an addition to the wallpaper design itself or they can be applied on a plain painted wall to add a patterned frame to the overall finish. Application methods vary according to where the border is being used.

## CEILING LEVEL

Ceiling level is the easiest place to hang a border because the ceiling junction can be used as a guideline when positioning the border itself. All borders should be pasted using proprietary border adhesive, which is stronger than normal paste and adheres much better to the wall surface.

1 Continue the ceiling colour slightly onto the wall surface so that if there are any undulations in the ceiling junction it will not be possible to see any wall colour above the border when it is applied – this gives the appearance of a precisely level ceiling edge.

2 Make a concertina out of the border in a similar way to when hanging wallpaper (see page 69). Apply the border using the ceiling junction as a guide to positioning the top edge of the border. Use a paper-hanging brush to smooth the border and remove any air bubbles from under its surface.

**Applying on wallpaper:** the advantage of applying a border on wallpaper is that it is usually easy to keep the border level by following a line in the actual pattern of the wallpaper. Where there is no ordered pattern to follow, draw a pencil guideline, as shown opposite.

5

# PICTURE AND DADO RAILS

Applying a border in one of the central areas of a wall is a simple process as long as the border is kept precisely level. When dealing with internal corners, never try to bend a single length around the corner as it will invariably shrink slightly as it dries and pull away from the corner junction. Use a single length of border per wall; join each length, matching the pattern along the junction.

1 Make a pencil mark on the wall at the required level and use a spirit level to draw a line around the entire perimeter of the room.

2 Use the pencil line as a guide for hanging the border. Crease the border firmly into the corner and trim it so that it overlaps slightly onto the adjacent wall.

3 Apply a second length of border so that it overlaps onto the first, taking care to match the pattern precisely. Draw a pencil guideline along the junction, peel the border back and trim with scissors.

4 Smooth the border back in place and remove the excess paste with a clean, damp sponge.

## TRIMMING CORNERS

Always trim the wallpaper at the corner with scissors. Don't use a craft knife as the blade could cut through both strips of border then, once the border is brushed back in place, the cut in both strips would reveal the wall colour below.

5

# COMBINING PAPERS

R ather than using just one wallpaper to decorate a room, it is possible to combine different papers to create an interesting and varied effect. Many manufacturers produce papers with this idea in mind and coordinate borders to be used with specific papers. You can either follow their guidelines or you can create your own individual schemes.

Using a border divide: using two different papers on the same wall surface requires some sort of border to divide the two patterns. A paper border acts as an ideal dado rail, separating the designs while adding a decorative feature.

Solid borders: a solid wooden dado rail can be used to divide different papers. This provides a pronounced finish and a clear-cut edge to both the wallpapers.

Framing: borders and wallpaper can be combined to create framed areas along a wall surface. The technique for creating mitre joins in borders is explained on page 111.

5

# COMBINING PAPER AND PAINT

*A successful decorative finish depends on a good combination of colour and design. By blending paper and paint together you can produce a very attractive and balanced decorative scheme. Texture and colour can both produce stunning results, and by combining the mediums of paint and paper, the options for experimentation are increased. There are many ways in which they can be combined and this chapter illustrates just a few of them, so you can go on to develop your own original ideas for all kinds of interesting, and unique, finishes.*

# WHAT TO USE WHERE

D ifferent paint and paper combinations can be used in particular areas of the home to create highly decorative effects. However, it is worth bearing in mind that some combinations and effects are better suited to certain areas than others.

## SUITING DIFFERENT AREAS

- Stairwells: these tend to receive a lot of wear and tear at the lower levels but not at the top. This makes them an ideal area to have a solid dado rail dividing two papers, or to have paper above the rail and paint below. Then, when the bottom level begins to look worn, it can be redecorated while leaving the top level as it is.
- Child's bedroom: in a similar manner to stairwells, the bottom level of the wall surface tends to get damaged more quickly. Having a solid dado rail divide or a paper border means that the bottom level can be redecorated while leaving the top level untouched. Using a paint effect below the dado can also help to disguise blemishes and make the finish last as long as possible.
- Alcoves: these offer the opportunity to create a feature within a room, and can be treated differently to the rest of the decoration. If the main walls are wallpapered, the back of the alcoves can be painted a light colour. This gives the effect of greater depth and provides an ideal background for displaying ornaments.
- Paper panels: paper panels can be very effective on walls, but they are less common on wooden surfaces. However, panel doors offer the ideal

opportunity for using wallpaper in a different way as the central area of each panel can be wallpapered to match the walls while the rest of the door is painted to match the other woodwork in the room.
- Découpage: this technique involves cutting out attractive designs or shapes from wallpaper, or other sources, and sticking them to the wall to create a collage effect. It is a good way of faking images, which is normally the domain of *faux* or *trompe-l'œil* artists.
- Painted borders: using paint as a border is another alternative to a wooden dado rail or paper border. Painted borders can be applied at any level to produce a frame for a particular feature.

6

# PAINTABLE PAPERS

Textured and paintable papers are the crossover between the wallpapering and painting worlds. These types of paper usually have an embossed surface which adds depth to the finish once the paper is applied to the wall. The textured pattern is excellent for covering up rough wall surfaces as the undulations are taken up by the thick embossed nature of the paper. Some of these papers are left unpainted, although most will benefit from being painted in either light or dark colours.

**Keeping it simple:** a textured, patterned paper can be painted a light colour while still showing off the depth in design. Using the paper up to the dado level also breaks up the wall surface, providing greater character and impact.

**Adding colour:** textured papers can be painted bold colours to enhance their features while, at the same time, creating a very solid look. Painted with vinyl emulsion, this effect is very hard-wearing and easy to clean.

**Basic texture:** woodchip paper is the most common of all the textured papers, and is extremely good for covering rough walls. On its own, the effect can be quite ordinary, but with the right accessories, woodchip can become an integral part of a decorative scheme.

6

# HANGING TEXTURED PAPER

Textured papers are hung in a similar way to normal wallpaper, but with one or two subtle differences in technique. Because they are generally heavier, the soaking time (for paste to soak into the paper) for textured paper tends to be slightly longer, and the paste is normally mixed to a stronger consistency.

## EMBOSSED PAPERS

Embossed papers have a relief pattern that raises the design, giving a much greater feeling of depth to the paper finish. When applying these types of wallpaper, care must be taken not to flatten the relief pattern and damage the textured effect.

1 Check the ends of each roll of wallpaper to make sure that the edges are not damaged. This is more of a problem with heavily patterned or particularly textured papers. For this reason, it is always best to store rolls of embossed paper horizontally, to avoid crushing the roll edges.

2 Once the paper has been pasted and allowed to soak for the manufacturer's recommended time, apply it to the wall using a paper-hanging brush. Use firm brush strokes to remove air bubbles from under the paper surface, but take care not to overbrush and, therefore, crush the pattern relief, especially along the joins between lengths.

3 Use a pencil to draw a guideline along the ceiling and skirting board junctions. Pull the paper back and trim along the line with sharp scissors – a craft knife can be used for trimming, but the coarse texture of the paper tends to blunt the blade of the craft knife very quickly and a blunt blade can tear the paper. Smooth the paper back into place.

6

# WOODCHIP REPAIRS

Textured woodchip paper is ideal for rough walls because it covers and disguises imperfections in the surface. As with embossed papers, use scissors for trimming – the small pieces of wood fibre in the paper are difficult to cut through with a craft knife. The most versatile property of woodchip paper is that it is very easy to repair damaged areas simply by patching and repainting.

1 Use a scraper to remove the loosely stuck-down edges of the damaged area of woodchip paper. Be sure to remove all the loose paper so that the remaining edge is stuck firmly to the wall surface, otherwise any loose flaps may bubble once the repair is complete and paint has been applied

2 Cut a piece of woodchip paper slightly larger than the hole. Hold it against the damaged area, tearing around the circumference of the hole as accurately as possible. Take the time to follow the exact profile of the tear required, so that the patch will fit the hole.

3 Apply some paste to the patch and allow it to soak for the recommended time before sticking it in place on the wall. Use a paper-hanging brush to remove any air bubbles in the usual way. Wipe the area with a clean, damp sponge to remove any excess paste.

4 Once the repair has dried, paint the whole area. Pay particular attention to the edges of the patch to make sure that they are covered. Once the whole wall has been painted, the repair patch will be invisible to the naked eye.

6

# PAINT EFFECTS ON TEXTURED PAPER

Textured papers offer the opportunity to create excellent paint effects since the raised surface adds a further dimension to the finished product. Applying the effect to the high points will give an entirely different finish to applying it to the low points of the paper.

## COLOUR WIPING

Colour wiping is a method of colouring the low points of a textured paper. It gives the appearance of the base colour being ingrained with the glaze colour that is applied to create the effect. Use a vinyl silk emulsion as the base coat for this paint effect.

1 Apply the glaze generously in all directions across the surface of the textured paper.

2 Use a clean damp sponge to wipe down the paper in long vertical sweeps. This technique is best used on papers with a dominant vertical pattern, as shown here; however, for an all-over design, the sponge can be wiped across the surface of the paper in any direction.

### LEAVING THE PEAKS
The finished effect leaves the peaks on the textured wallpaper surface clear of glaze, so the base-coat colour shows clearly on these raised areas.

## COLOUR HIGHLIGHTING

The aim of highlighting is to accentuate the peaks in the paper with the glaze colour, rather than the troughs. The glaze is applied to the peaks and left in place, rather than being wiped away as with the colour wiping technique. A base coat of vinyl silk emulsion should be used for this effect as well.

1  Once the brush has been dipped in glaze, dry off the excess from the bristles with a clean cloth.

2  Use light, sweeping, horizontal strokes across the surface of the paper, just allowing the bristles to touch the top of the relief pattern.

3  Build up the depth of colour to the level you require before moving onto the next area on the paper surface.

### TEXTURE WITH HEIGHT AND DEPTH
The result looks as if the paper texture has both height and depth – quite different from the effect of colour wiping, even though the same glaze, paper and base coat have been used to achieve this effect.

6

# HANGING WALL PANELS

W all panels are thicker than wallpaper and require a heavy-duty paste in order to stick them to the wall. To produce the best possible finish, walls should also be lined before applying the panels. Most panels are designed to be applied at dado level around a room. It is usually possible to apply whole panels and reduce the need for cutting and trimming.

1 Soak the back of the wall panel with warm water, and leave for 20 minutes before applying paste. This allows the panel to expand, and will prevent any bubbles appearing in its surface once applied to the wall.

2 Apply paste generously to the panel, ensuring that it covers all areas, including the edges.

3 Apply the panel to the wall, ideally starting in an internal corner. Use a spirit level to ensure that the panel is vertical.

4 Brush out any air bubbles in the paper using a paper-hanging brush. Take care not to damage the panel surface during this process.

6

5 Once one wall is complete, begin the adjacent wall. Start and, therefore, join, the design at the internal corner.

6 Run a bead of decorator's caulk along internal corners to produce a perfect neat finish.

## CUTTING REQUIREMENTS

When smaller panels are required, use a straight edge and craft knife to cut the panel to the correct size before pasting.

## ADDING BORDERS

You can enhance the wall panel effect by adding a border or dado trim above it. Paper borders are not ideal for this purpose as they tend to be overshadowed by the depth of the wall panels themselves. The solution is to use a border made from the same heavy-duty material as the panels. This should be applied using the same adhesive as that used for the wall panels. The alternative option is to apply a wooden dado trim around the top of the wall panels. This provides a very solid and substantial edge to the complete panel effect. A wooden dado trim can either be painted or stained, according to personal taste.

6

# PAINT EFFECTS ON WALL PANELS

W all panels can be painted in a single colour or they can be used for various paint effects. In the example below, an impressive verdigris effect has been created by colour wiping and highlighting.

1 The texture of wall panels means that both colour-wiping and highlighting techniques are ideal to use on them. Clean all the panels with white spirit, then allow them to dry before applying any paint. With ornate panel textures, such as the one shown here, pay particular attention to all the details in the pattern, so that all impurities are removed from the surface. Wear protective gloves to protect your hands.

2 Apply an oil-based undercoat to seal and prime the panels, taking care to cover them evenly and not to create any drips or runs across the intricate surface of the panels. Use a gentle, swirling motion with the bristles of the brush to make sure that you get the paint into all the fine details of the design. Further coats of paint on the panels can be water-based.

3 A pale-green base coat is the ideal colour to begin a verdigris effect. As with the undercoat, it should be applied all over the wall-panel surface. Water-based emulsion paint is the best choice. It means that two coats can be applied in one day. Once the second coat is dry, you can begin applying the verdigris effect.

6

4 Load a mini-roller with dark green paint and remove the excess on a scrap piece of paper. Run the roller very gently across the panel surface, just touching the high points and peaks of the pattern. Do not apply too much pressure, otherwise the paint will be forced into the deeper troughs that make up the texture of the panel.

5 Using the same technique as in step 4, add a further coat of paint – with a rusty red being the ideal choice of colour. Again, take care not to apply too much pressure. Try to vary the intensity of the colour by applying slightly more in some places than in others.

6 Mix up a dark green glaze and brush it over the entire panel surface, giving a translucent top coat to the finished effect. Make sure that the entire surface is evenly coated.

### THE VERDIGRIS EFFECT
The finished panel effect can be quite stunning, providing the perfect background for furniture and ornaments alike. Further coats of glaze can be applied to create greater depth and texture.

6

# FRAMING WITH BORDERS

As well as creating a decorative edge, borders can be used to very good effect as frames. You can use paint or paper borders to highlight the overall decoration in a room, or they can be used on a smaller scale to accentuate particular features.

## PAINTED BORDERS

Using paint to act as a frame is a common concept – in effect, painted skirting boards and architraves act as the border around walls in most rooms in the house. However, the framed effect can be made more striking by using stencils specifically designed and made for use as a continuous painted border. Using borders in a less obvious position, such as around the skirting board, can create an excellent effect, especially if continued along corner junctions and next to the ceiling so that the entire wall is framed.

1 Use masking tape to stick the stencil to the wall above the skirting. Make sure that it is level before applying any paint with a stencil brush.

2 Use a second colour to add texture to the stencilled border.

3 Move the stencil along and use the last section in the design as a guide for repositioning the stencil on the wall, ready for the next length of border to be stencilled in.

6

# PAPER BORDERS

Paper borders can be just as effective as paint in framing walls or areas such as the door architrave, as shown below. In addition to the normal technique for applying a border, it is necessary to mitre joins in the border so that the direction can be changed to produce square 90 degree corners. Choose the borders carefully when planning to mitre joins, as some border patterns are not suitable for doing this.

1 Apply two lengths of border so that they overlap at the corner of the door architrave. When cutting the lengths, allow a generous amount for the overlap. This allows you plenty of room to manoeuvre the two strips into the best possible position for matching the pattern and mitring the corner.

2 Use a craft knife to cut through the overlap at a diagonal angle, beginning at the corner of the door architrave and finishing at the corner cross section of the two lengths of border. Take care to avoid cutting the painted wall with the craft knife.

3 Peel back both strips of border and remove the excess pieces of paper created by the diagonal cut. These two pieces are now excess to requirements and can be discarded.

4 Smooth the two strips back into position to produce a neat, mitred join. Remove excess paste with a clean, damp sponge. Use the same technique to deal with the opposite architrave corner.

6

# INDEX

All illustrations by Chris Forsey. All photographs by Tim Ridley except for the following pages:

l = left, r = right, c = centre, t = top, b = bottom

Page 5 Elizabeth Whiting & Associates; 6t Elizabeth Whiting & Associates; 7t Elizabeth Whiting & Associates; 8t Elizabeth Whiting & Associates; 8c Elizabeth Whiting & Associates; 13t Elizabeth Whiting & Associates, 13c Elizabeth Whiting & Associates; 66t Nick Huggins/Houses & Interiors; 66c Elizabeth Whiting & Associates, 66b Elizabeth Whiting & Associates; 98t Elizabeth Whiting & Associates, 98c Elizabeth Whiting & Associates; 101t Elizabeth Whiting & Associates, 101c Elizabeth Whiting & Associates, 101b Elizabeth Whiting & Associates.